The History and Beliefs of Old Catholicism and the Old Catholic Church of North America

"De Oppresso Liber"

Rt. Rev. Michael NeSmith, D.Div.

Doctoral Dissertation for St. Michael's Seminary

© 2007 St. Michael's Seminary
2nd edition

All rights reserved. No part of this publication may be reproduced, stored in a retrieval system, or transmitted in any form or by any means, electronic, mechanical, photocopying, recording, or otherwise, without the prior permission of the copyright owner.

St. Michael's Seminary
PO Box, 260473
Tampa, Florida 33685

Printed in the United States of America

ISBN 978-0-6151-7849-3

Table of Contents

Introduction..5

Section I	Ecclesiology of the Early Church...	7
	Ecclesiology..	7
	What Makes a Church Catholic...................................	7
	The Infallible church – Ecumenical Councils	9
	Seven Ecumenical Councils..	10
Section II	Beliefs of the Early Church...	11
	Original Sin...	11
	Beliefs – Blessed Virgin Mary...................................	12
	Beliefs – Other Differences.......................................	12
Section III	Old Catholics in Europe..	14
	The Great Schism..	14
	The Ever Changing Western Church..........................	14
	Churches of Willibrord – France...............................	15
	Churches of Willibrord – Netherlands.......................	17
	The Apex of the Conflict: Power of the Pope.................	17
	European Old Catholic Beliefs.................................	19
	14 Theses of the Old Catholic Union.........................	19
	Declaration of Utrecht	19
Section IV	Old Catholicism Comes to the New World...........................	22
	Independent Movement Today...............................	22
	Apostolic Succession...	22
	Bishop Arnold Harris Mathew................................	23
	Bishop Joseph Rene' Vilatte....................................	23
	Relations with Utrecht...	23
	Common traits of the Churches	24
	Old Roman Catholic..	24
	Independent Catholic..	24
	Old Catholics...	24
Section V	The Old Catholic Church of North America.........................	26
	Beliefs of OCCNA..	26
	Liturgy of the OCCNA...	26
	Frequently Asked Questions...................................	26
	Short Summary of the Faith....................................	28
	God...	28
	Jesus Christ...	28
	Holy Spirit...	29
	Sin...	29
	Salvation...	29
	Baptism...	29

New Birth	30
Justification	30
Sanctification	30
The Bible	30
Worship	30
Liturgy	31
Eucharist	31
Communion of Saints	31
Confession	31
Mary	31
Prayer to the Saints	32
Apostolic Succession	32
Councils of the Church	32
Creed	32
Spiritual Gifts	33
Second Coming	33
Heaven	33
Hell	33
Creation	33
Bibliography	34
Bulls Unigenitus (Complete Text)	35
Bull for Consecration of Bishop Vilatte	40
Place of the Old Catholics in the Work of Unity	41
New Schaff-Herzog Encyclopedia of Religion – Old Catholics	43

Introduction

First I would like to explain that in writing this paper I have attempted to use only sources that would be deemed credible and acceptable by any institution of higher learning. The sources I used consist of encyclopedias, the Old Catholic Churches of Europe (Utrecht Union), and publications accepted as valid by scholars. A complete listing of the texts used is in the bibliography and I would suggest that any individual seeking to understand Old Catholicism add them to their personal library. In addition there is an appendix that contains not only copies of documents referenced in this text but also additional historical documents pertaining to the subject

The purpose of this work is to provide the reader with not only the historical time frame of the development of the Old Catholic faith, but also to provide a basic understanding of the events and reasons that led to the separation from the Roman Communion. In order to convey this level of understanding we must first look at the beginning of the Christian Church itself, for it was the ecclesiology and theology of the early Church that was proclaimed to, and accepted by, the people in what is now the Netherlands and France. It is my opinion if one does not seek to understand the ecclesiology and beliefs of what could be called our "birth" church then one often misses the true reason for the decision to separate from Rome, which was to return "home".

I challenge the reader that in order to truly understand Old Catholicism one must "unlearn" much of what they know about the Christian Church and Faith of this time. We must clear our minds of all the institutional teachings, doctrines, and dogmas that make up the Church that most are familiar with, and mentally return to a time when the thousands of Protestant Churches did not exist; to a time when the Roman Communion did not claim supremacy; to a time before the Reformation; to a time in the life of the Church prior to the great schism of 1054 when there was no "Roman" and "Orthodox"; to a time when there was the One Holy Catholic and Apostolic Church.

To begin our understanding of Old Catholicism it is essential that we look back to the very first centuries as Christianity began to spread among the known world and remember that Jesus left the Early Church with no new law, no new principles, and no written books. He sent out his apostles to teach and spread the "good news" throughout the world *(Mk. 16:15)*. He provided them with sacraments through which the grace of God could flow to all mankind *(Mat. 28: 19-20)*.

His crucifixion, death, and resurrection were the cornerstone of the faith *(1 Cor. 15: 12-14)*. The Early Church was a group of people who accepted Jesus as leader and guide *(Heb. 4: 14-16)*.

It was during this time while the Church was one and undivided and of one mind that the Anglo-Saxon monk Willibrord (*see insert*) missionized the area of Europe now known as the Netherlands and France.

It was this earlier "undivided" Christianity that was taught to the people in this part of the world and it is that "undivided" Church that Old Catholics seek to restore. So let us proceed by exploring the ecclesiology and theology of that era so that we might better understand what Old Catholicism is. And of perhaps even greater importance what Old Catholicism in not.

St. Willibrord

Apostle of Frisia, Netherlands, a missionary archbishop. Born in Northumbria, England, circa 658, he studied at Ripon monastery under St. Wilfrid and spent twelve years studying in Ireland at the abbey of Rathmelsigi (most likely Mellifont, County Louth) under Sts. Egbert and Wigbert. After receiving ordination and extensive training in the field of the missions, he set out about 690 with a dozen companions for Frisia, or Friesland. In 693, he went to Rome to seek papal approval for his labors, Pope Sergius I (r. 687-701) gave his full approbation and, during Willibrord's second Roman visit, the pontiff consecrated him archbishop to the Frisians, in 696, with his see at Utrecht.

Source: *Patron Saints Index* - http://www.catholic-forum.com/saints/indexsnt.htm

Section I
The Ecclesiology of the Early Church

Ecclesiology

The American Heritage Dictionary of the English Language, Fourth Edition provides the following definitions for the word ecclesiology:
1. *The branch of theology that is concerned with the nature, constitution, and functions of a church.*
2. *The study of ecclesiastical architecture and ornamentation.*

It is the first definition that we are interested in as we begin to explore the Church of St. Willibrord. I beg the reader to understand that for the sake of time I have not gone into great detail concerning ecclesiology or beliefs. Instead I have endeavored to provide enough material to present the both basics of the faith of the Early Church and serve as introduction to Old Catholicism. It is my hope and prayer that the reader will begin to explore and seek to understand our faith as Old Catholics. Let us now begin our short study of Early Church Ecclesiology.

What Makes a Church Catholic?

The definition of the word *catholic* according to the Catholic Encyclopedia[1] is this; *Catholic* (*katholikos* from *katholou*) "throughout the whole -, i.e., universal".

Ewells Theological Dictionary says this about the word *catholic*:
> *This is its meaning in the first occurrence in a Christian setting, "Wherever Jesus Christ is, there is the catholic church" (Ignatius Smyr. 8:2). Here the contrast with the local congregation makes the meaning "universal" mandatory. Justin Martyr would speak of the "catholic" resurrection, which he explains as meaning the resurrection of all men (Dialogues lxxxi). When the term begins to appear in the Apostles' Creed, "the holy catholic church" (AD. 450), as it had earlier appeared in the Nicene, "one holy catholic and apostolic church", it retains the sense of universality and thus accents the unity of the church in spite of its wide diffusion.*

"*Wherever Jesus Christ is, there is the catholic church*" and "*unity in spite of wide diffusion*". This understanding of what is catholic does not fit very well with the understanding of many modern day Christians, and especially with the current teaching of the Roman Communion. The Roman Church proclaims that it is the only "catholic" church and that it alone possesses the completeness of Christ. So well has this misconception been taught that most people automatically associate the word catholic to mean Roman Catholic. In fact, most dictionaries will provide a definition for the word "catholic" as one that is a member of the Roman Catholic Church and/or pertaining to the Roman Catholic Church. But, what did it mean in the early Church to be catholic, to be part of the "one holy catholic and apostolic church"? In order to answer this question let's look at the structure and nature of a local church in the first centuries of Christianity.

According to St. Paul, the Apostles went about proclaiming the gospel, establishing communities of worshippers, and appointing and ordaining leaders in the local churches *(Titus 1:5-7)*. Elsewhere in the New Testament St. Paul makes reference to the offices of bishop and deacon *(Phil. 1:1, 1Tim. 1:3-16)*. The structure of the leadership of the Early Church is even more defined in a letter written by St. Clement, the third bishop of Rome, around A.D. 96. As you can see from the excerpt of the letter below St. Clement makes reference to Bishops, presbyters (priests), levites (deacons), and the laity. The writings clearly indicate that a four-fold church structure was in place at this time.

> *He commanded us to celebrate sacrifices and services, and that it should not be thoughtlessly or disorderly, but at fixed times and hours. He has Himself fixed by his supreme will the places and persons whom He desires for these celebrations, in order that all things may be done piously according to His good pleasure, and be acceptable to His will... For to the high priest his proper ministrations are allotted, and to the priest the proper place has been appointed, and on levites their proper services have been imposed. The layman is bound by ordnances for the laity.*[2]

The writings of Saint Justin in the middle of the second century refer to the bishop as the "President" of the brethren. St. Justin described the church structure as been governed by a single person and that person being the Bishop. Based on all the evidence from the early Fathers the office of bishop was not jointly held (as with the Pope) but it was understood that a single Bishop was and is, the presiding presbyter, pastor, and governs the local church.

> *At the end of the prayers we embrace each other with a kiss. Then bread is brought to the President of the brethren, and a cup of water and wine. This he takes, and offers praise and glory to the Father of all, through the name of His Son and of the Holy Spirit; and he gives thanks at length the for our being granted the gifts at his hand. When he has finished the prayers and the thanksgiving all the people present give their assent with "amen", a Hebrew word signifying, "So be it". When the president has given thanks and all the people have assented, those whom we call "deacons" give a portion of the bread over which thanksgiving has been offered, and of the wine and water, to each of those who are present; and they carry them away to those who are absent.*[3]

Our current the structure and terminology of the threefold ministry can be accredited to St. Ignatius of Antioch when he wrote:

> *Take great care to keep one Eucharist. For there is one flesh of our Lord Jesus Christ and one cup to unite us by His blood; one sanctuary, as there is one bishop, together with the presbytery, and the deacons, my fellow-servants. Thus all of your acts may be done according to God's will.*[4]

St. Ignatius is also the first person to use the adjective "catholic" in regard to the Church. As we can see from the previous texts the structure of the local church (diocese), presided over by the bishop, is the whole, complete, "*catholic*" Church. And as such the fullness of Christ was, and is manifested both in and through each local diocese and church. This does not mean that the church was not universal for each Communion (Church) shared a common faith, sacraments, and Gospel with the other churches and dioceses. The unity between the Churches was expressed by intercommunion and concelebration and not by any single ruling individual or diocese.

I realize that such thinking is diametrically opposed to the current teaching of the Roman Church, which is, that the Pope as the sole successor of Peter has universal primacy of jurisdiction over the ecumenical Church. This claim is dependent upon the notion that that universal Church rather than the diocese (local) Church is the Catholic Church. Concerning this notion let's examine two of the writings of Cyprian.

> *You should know that the bishop is in the Church, and the Church is in the bishop. If anyone is not with the bishop, he is not in the Church.*
>
> And
>
> *Peter-the one the Lord chose first and upon whom built his church-did not in insolently claim anything to himself. Nor did he arrogantly assume anything when Paul later disputed him about circumcision. He did not say that he held primacy and that he needed to be obeyed by novices and those lately come!*[5]

As evidenced by the previous writings (not to mention many other documents and writings) the train of thought that any one Bishop had a position of "universal primacy of jurisdiction" simply cannot be supported. In fact, it is difficult to find a true church scholar in this day and time that will not admit that the Popes role in the early church was a position of honor. He [the Pope] was recognized as being first among equals (as all Bishops were considered to be equal in their authority) and as such had no absolute authority over other Bishops, nor did any single bishop have the authority to declare dogmas binding on all Churches. In short, for the first few centuries it was accepted that each diocese (church) with its Bishop was in itself fully "catholic" and that in the Early Church there was no universal primacy of jurisdiction

The Infallible Church - The Ecumenical Councils

Well then, one cannot help but wonder if all Bishops are equal how did the Church make doctrinal decisions about the faith?

As the church continued to grow it became necessary to clarify teaching and beliefs so that the faith could be passed down from generation to generation without compromising the truth.

To resolve problems and answer questions concerning what was Orthodox (right teaching) the Early Church would come together in council in the same example provided in the New Testament in the Book of Acts. *(Acts chapter 1: 21-25, Acts 4:31-37, Acts 6:2, Acts 11:2-3, Acts 15:29, Acts 21:18)*. It was also understood that for a council (and it decisions) to be truly accepted the council must be Ecumenical in nature and include representatives from all Churches (Communions) over which the Sees of the five great Bishops of Christendom presided.

These Bishops represented the important cities of Jerusalem, Antioch, Constantinople, Alexandria and Rome. They were known as patriarchs in whom the Church of the ancients recognized each as been equal in authority and office. As mentioned earlier the bishop of Rome was acknowledged as the successor of Peter, however the position was one of honor and not primacy. It was accepted without question that the Infallibility of the Church lie within the decisions of the council and not with any one bishop or individual church. Additionally, it must be emphasized that the decisions of such a council alone do not denote infallibility – it is the acceptance by the Church *(consensus Ecclesiae)* that such decisions / councils can be said to be infallible.

To date the Old Catholic Church recognizes that there have been only seven such councils *(see inset)*. These councils occurred before the Great Schism of 1054. It is from the Ecumenical Councils that the basic Dogmas (Creeds and Beliefs/Traditions) common to all Catholics and to most Christians are derived.

I cannot emphasize enough the importance of an understanding and acceptance of the decisions of the Ecumenical Councils. The impact of the Councils goes far beyond simply providing guidance and clarifying teachings and beliefs.

The Councils provide for us the Dogmas of the Church as stated in the Creeds, condemn forever heresies, which continue to arise in various Christian denominations even toady, and it was the Church in Council that also selected the Canon of the New Testament. Therefore, it is easy to see that to reject or accept the infallibility of either Scripture, Dogmas, or Ecumenical Council is to accept or reject all three. I strongly recommend that all clergy take the time to read and study the Councils with a focus on the dogmatic Canons of each.

The text by Fr. Michael Pomazansky, *Orthodox Dogmatic Theology A Concise Exposition 2nd Edition*, (Jordanville, NY., Holy Trinity Monastery, 1997 is a good place to begin understanding the beliefs of the Early Church.

The Seven Ecumenical Councils

First Ecumenical Council - Nicea, Asia Minor, 325 A.D.
- Formulated the First Part of the Creed. Defining the divinity of the Son of God.

Second Ecumenical Council - Constantinople, 381 A.D.
- Formulated the Second Part of the Creed, defining the divinity of the Holy Spirit.

Third Ecumenical Council - Ephesus, Asia Minor, 431A.D.
- Defined Christ as the Incarnate Word of God and Mary as Theotokos.

Fourth Ecumenical Council - Chalcedon, Asia Minor, 451A.D.
- Defined Christ as Perfect God and Perfect God and Perfect Man in One Person.

Fifth Ecumenical Council - Constantinople II, 553 A.D.
- Reconfirmed the Doctrines of the Trinity and Christ.

Sixth Ecumenical Council - Constantinople III, 680 A.D.
- Affirmed the True Humanity of Jesus by insisting upon the reality of His Human will and action. (Qinisext Council (Trullo) – Constantinople, 692 A.D.
- Completed the 5th and 6th Ecumenical Councils)

Seventh Ecumenical Council - Nicea, Asia Minor, 787 A.D.
- Affirmed the propriety of icons as genuine expressions of the Christian Faith.

Source: *Greek Orthodox Church* http://www.goholycross.org/studies/councils.html#Seven

Section II
The Beliefs of the Early Church

In order to better fully understand the reason for the conflict between the Roman Church and the Churches founded by Willibrord we must understand some of the beliefs of the Early Church as compared to the same beliefs as proclaimed by the Roman Church in the early 18th century. In each of these particular areas of teaching the magisterium of Rome is vastly different from that of the Early Church and the church of St. Willibrord with the end result being a schism.

It is of particular importance that the reader understand the teachings of the Early Church pertaining to the Fall of Man (original sin), The Blessed Virgin Mary, and the position of the Bishop of Rome as a See of honor and not primacy in order to understand both the History and Beliefs of Old Catholics.

Original Sin

Therefore as sin came into the world through one man and death through sin, and so death spread to all men because all men sinned' *(Rom.5: 12)*. To the early Church original sin meant that our human nature has been infected by sin in general as a result of Adam and Eve's choice. As St Cyril of Alexandria states human nature itself has *'fallen ill with sin'*; thus we all share Adam's sin as we all share his nature [11]. St Macarius of Egypt speaks of *'a leaven of evil passions'* and of *'secret impurity and the abiding darkness of passions'*, which have entered into our nature in spite of our original purity [ibid]. The Early Church did not teach that man inherited the *guilt* of Adams sin, as was later taught by St. Augustine, but rather the *effects* of that sin, namely a nature enslaved to corruption and death. In short we are all born with a sinful nature into a sinful world (result of Adams sin) but not with the actual guilt (stain) of the actions of Adam.

This leads to a very profound and distinct difference between the current teaching by many churches (including the Roman Church) and the Old Catholic and Orthodox Churches as to why Jesus became man.

According to Roman Catholic theology, God became man in order to satisfy divine Justice, which was offended by the sin of Adam. Only Christ, Who was God and man, could pay this "debt", and He pays the debt by dying on the Cross. His death makes up for what Adam had done; the offense is removed. God is no longer angry with man.

Following the holy Fathers, Old Catholic like the Orthodox teach that Christ, on the Cross, gave "His life a ransom for many" (Matt. 20:28). "For even the Son of man came not to be served, but to serve, and to give His life a ransom for many" (Mark 10:45). The "ransom" is paid to the grave. As the Lord revealed to the Prophet Hosea (Hosea 13:14), "I will ransom them (us) from the power of the grave, I will redeem them from death." In a sense, He pays the ransom to the devil who has the keeper of the grave and holds the power of death (Heb. 2:14). While this at first glance sounds the same there is a great difference in that Old Catholic and Orthodox teaching in that the man Christ voluntarily gave Himself on the Cross. He died for all ("a ransom for many" or "the many") because of His great love for mankind not as an act of fulfillment of divine justice. It is because of His freely chosen act of sacrifice / love and resurrection from the grave that death was conquered and as such the human race is redeemed from the grave, from the devil. Free of the devil is to be free of death and sin. In short Jesus was and is the Great Physician – the Great Healer of the sickness of sin and its consequences.

In closing, to some this might seem to the reader a "splitting of theological hairs" and of not much importance to anyone except a theologian. However, it is from the acceptance of the belief that all people inherit the "stain" of Adam that the Roman Church had to formulate an ever-increasing series of doctrines and dogmas one of which was the Dogma of the Immaculate Conception which, as we will discuss later, is one of the key issues resulting in the schism between Old Catholics and Roman Catholics.

Beliefs – The Blessed Virgin Mary

At the time of St. Willibrord there were two doctrines about our Lord's Mother that were binding on all Christians. The first is that when her son Jesus was born she was a virgin, which is an article of the Nicene Creed. The second is that she is rightly called Theotokos (God - Bearer), which was accepted by all the Churches and declared by the General Council of Ephesus in the year A.D. 431.

The Rev. C. B. Moss in his book, *The Old Catholic Movement Its History and Origins 2nd Edition* has this to say about these two dogmas and about the veneration of the Blessed Virgin. While this text is written to express Anglican Theology it also conveys the beliefs of the Early Church, as well as those of Old Catholics, about these dogmas.

The Virgin Birth, and the Title Theotokos

The Anglican churches maintain the fundamental principle that nothing may be taught as necessary to salvation but that which may be found in or proved by Holy Scripture. According to this principle there are two dogmas, and only two, which refer to the Blessed Virgin Mary; and these two are binding on all members of the Church. They are the dogma of the Virgin Birth, that at the time of our Lord's birth His mother was a Virgin, and He had no earthly father; and the dogma that the Blessed Virgin is rightly called Theotókos, accepted by the Council of Ephesus. The first is based on the Gospels, St. Matt. 1:20 and St. Luke 1:35; the evidence for it will be given (in pp 108-115 of original book).

The second is a necessary deduction from St. John 1:14. We accept it, not merely because the Council of Ephesus defined it, still less because Pope Celestine confirmed that definition, but because the whole Church has decided that the Council of Ephesus was right, and that what it defined had always been the belief of the Church.

Value of the Veneration of the Blessed Virgin

The love and reverence given by all Christians, until the Reformation, to our Lord's Mother have been of the highest spiritual and moral value. They have inspired the ideal of chivalry towards all women. They have supported the teaching of St. Paul that in Christ men and women are equal. They have strengthened, as perhaps nothing else could have done, personal purity and the ideal of the Christian home. They are one of the most precious parts of Christian tradition, and the sects which have cast them away have suffered immeasurable loss. (IV)

Beliefs – Other Differences

At this time I would like to note that the understating of Original Sin and the rejection of the Dogma of the Immaculate Conception are not the only differences separating Old Catholics and Roman Catholics. There are many other beliefs and practices common to the Roman Church of today that were foreign to the Early Church, and the Churches of St. Willibrord. Some of these dogmas, beliefs, and practices are: Papal Infallibility, Purgatory, Indulgences, The Mass as Immolation, Transubstantiation, Clerical Celibacy, Dogma of the Assumption, Mary as Co-Redemptrix, use of a Rosary, and the entire method of canonization of Saints.

In closing this section I hope that I have at least fueled the desire of the reader to research and broaden their understanding and knowledge of the Early Church for I firmly believe that in order to purge the heresies of the modern church one must return to and understand the teachings of the Early Church. For it is through knowledge of the Early Church that one is able to separate those non-universal beliefs that have been imbedded into our thoughts and memory by our birth church be it Roman or other. This precept is best stated by St. Vincent of Lerins in his rule of faith which says: *"Id teneamus, quod ubique, quod semper, quod ab omnibus creditum est; hoc est etenim vere proprieque catholicum."* (Hold fast that faith which has been believed everywhere [universally], always, and by all.)

Section III
Old Catholics in Europe

The Great Schism

As the Church grew so did its power in the world. And as the power the Church held not only over matters of faith but also matters of state. Eventually the Roman Church began to exercise more and more authority and dominance until in 1054 the Roman Churches claimed to have authority to change the wording of the Nicene Creed outside of Ecumenical Council. It was at this time that the words *"from the Son"* (*Filioque*) were added to the section of the Creed that provided the teachings / dogmas concerning the Holy Spirit and His place in the Triune Godhead.

I will not even begin to debate the theological implication of this addition as there have been countless books written and the debate is just as intense to this day as it was almost one thousand years ago. Instead I will say that all the "catholic" churches (including the Roman Church) had previously agreed that no one church had the authority to change or alter the creed, decisions of a council, or declare any belief as binding outside of full council. So it was this very action that was the "straw that broke the camels back" so to speak and led to the schism of 1054.

It was at this point in history that the supremacy of the Pope was firmly established in the Roman Catholic Church. There were now two separate bodies of Christians. The Roman Catholic Church, which was predominant in the western part of the world, and the Orthodox Church, which was predominant in the eastern world. The Roman Catholic Church focused more on a centralized control and the supremacy of the Pope over the Church. The Orthodox Church focused more on the autonomy of each bishop and still carried on the traditions and teachings of the Early Church.

The Ever Changing Western Church

During the Middle Ages the Roman Church found herself increasingly burdened with secular responsibility in addition to its religious responsibilities. The Pope was not only the head of the Church but had also become a secular ruler and had the authority to enact taxes, imprison lawbreakers, and even fight wars.
Rather than going into a great amount of detail about the problems with the Roman Catholic Church during the Middle Ages I think it's safe to say that all readers would recognize that during this time in history the Roman Church began to overstep its authority and became filled with corrupt and immoral leaders. Eventually a cry for

reform went out and in 1414 the Roman Church convened the Council of Constance in an attempt to reform and return to the teachings and beliefs of the Early Church.

Unfortunately the council did not accomplish the task it set out to do. With this failure of reformation from within reformation came from without. The Protestant Reformation and subsequent Schism from the Church began under the leadership of Martin Luther. In response the Roman Catholic Church once again attempted to both reform itself and check the now fast growing Protestant movement with the Council of Trent (1545-1563). While this council did much to reform the Catholic Church, such abolishing the sale of indulgences, the council also declared that tradition should be made equal with scripture and that the Pope having the power to decide what is true tradition could therefore add new Dogmas to the Catholic Faith. The end result of the council was to further separate the churches rather than to unite. Christendom was now divided into three groups (Roman, Orthodox, and Protestant).

It is of utmost importance for the reader to understand that the Roman Church, which was placing greater emphasis on the authority of the Pope, was the voice of the "Catholic" faith in the western world. The Orthodox Churches, which held fast to the teachings and traditions of the Early Church, had remained in the East and was largely unknown to Christians in the West. And now the third group of the Protestant reformers who in their zeal to battle Papal Supremacy had in effect abandoned all of the Early Tradition and focused increasingly on Scripture alone (Sola Scripture).
Simultaneous to, and in the midst of all of this controversy and turmoil, there existed within the Roman Catholic Church small pockets of Catholics that while Western in their liturgy and traditions still adhered to the teachings and faith of the Early Church.

These were the Catholics in the areas of Europe that had been missionized by St. Willibrord. In essence, there were two distinctly different theologies existing in the Roman Church at the same time. Each theology had its separate group of leaders.

The leaders of the first of these two groups were the Jesuits. Ignatius Loyola founded this great order with the purpose of forming a kind of army for propagating the faith. The order was to be at the absolute disposal of the Pope to whom each member took a special vow of obedience. The Jesuits were the champions of the most extreme claims of the Papacy. They held that the Church was a society wholly distinct from the state, and completely controlled in all its parts by the Pope. They denied that any authority within the Church could exist which what was not derived from the supreme authority, the Pope. They therefore tried to destroy all remains of any Episcopal or national independence from Rome.

The second group was made up of those within the Roman Catholic Church that clung to the teachings and traditions of the Early Church as taught by St. Willibrord. It was out of this group that the Old Catholic church had its beginning. There were two predominant churches / dioceses that railed against the increasing power of the Pope and Rome. They were the Jansenist Church of France and the See of Utrecht in the Netherlands. As we know both of these groups were destined to fail in their attempt to keep Roman Church from finally and completely abandoning the ways of the Early Church.

The Churches of Willibrord - France
First let us examine the plight of the French Church. Both the Catholic Church in France and the King of France refused to accept the articles taught by the Jesuits. These articles [12] stated that:

1) *The pope is infallible in judging on faith and morals.*
2) *In no case was there a council superior to the Pope.*

3) It belongs to the Pope to determine doubt questions, and to confirm or disallow the decision of all councils.

In response to these articles the French church replied that ecclesiastical jurisdiction belonged to the whole Church, and the authority of the Pope, as its ministerial head, was not over the Church as a whole, which as we know was the teaching of the Early Church.

Needless to say the debate and disagreement grew between the French Church and the Roman Pontiff. From the year 1662 through 1713 the battle over who would reign over the Church in France intensified.

Of key importance in the history of the Old Catholic Faith was the refusal of many Bishops, especially the Bishops of the Netherlands, to accept a Papal Bull, which is a special letter or document bearing the seal of the Pope[6], that condemned a work entitled, *Paschasius Quesnel* that was a collection of beliefs / propositions of the French Jansenist Church.

The Papal Bull *Unigenitus* was issued by Pope Clement XI on Sept. 8, 1713 (and upheld later by Popes Innocent XIII, Benedict XII, and Clement XII) and specifically lists and condemns some 101 items found in the *Paschasius Quesnel*. Below you will first find the declaration of condemnation of the *Paschasius Quesnel* as written in the *Bull Unigenitus*. Immediately following the statement of condemnation you will find a few of the teachings that were specifically condemned.
   (A complete copy of this document may be found in the appendix and may be found online at http://www.papalencyclicals.net/Clem11/c11unige.htm.)

Declaration of Condemnation:

"Declared and condemned as false, captious, evil-sounding, offensive to pious ears, scandalous, pernicious, rash, injurious to the Church and her practice, insulting not only to the Church but also the secular powers seditious, impious, blasphemous, suspected of heresy, and smacking of heresy itself, and, besides, favoring heretics and heresies, and also schisms, erroneous, close to heresy, many times condemned, and finally heretical, clearly renewing many heresies respectively and most especially those which are contained in the infamous propositions of Jansen, and indeed accepted in that sense in which these have been condemned."

Below you will find a few selected Teachings From the *Paschasius Quesnel* which were **condemned as being heretical** by the Bull Unigenitus:

73. What is the Church except an assembly of the sons of God abiding in His bosom, adopted in Christ, subsisting in His person, redeemed by His blood, living in His spirit, acting through His grace, and awaiting the grace of the future life?
74. The Church or the whole Christ has the Incarnate Word as head but all the saints as members
79. It is useful and necessary at all times, in all places, and for every kind of person, to study and to know the spirit, the piety, and the mysteries of Sacred Scripture.
80. The reading of Sacred Scripture is for all.
82. The Lord's Day ought to be sanctified by Christians with readings of pious works and above all of the Holy Scriptures. It is harmful for a Christian to wish to withdraw from this reading.
83. It is an illusion to persuade oneself that knowledge of the mysteries of religion should not be communicated to women by the reading of Sacred Scriptures. Not from the simplicity of women, but from the proud knowledge of men has arisen the abuse of the Scriptures and have heresies been born.
84. To snatch away from the hands of Christians the New Testament, or to hold it closed against them by taking away from them the means of understanding it, is to close for them the mouth of Christ.

85. To forbid Christians to read Sacred Scripture, especially the Gospels, is to forbid the use of light to the sons of light, and to cause them to suffer a kind of excommunication.
86. To snatch from the simple people this consolation of joining their voice to the voice of the whole Church is a custom contrary to the apostolic practice and to the intention of God.
91. The fear of an unjust excommunication should never hinder us from fulfilling our duty; never are we separated from the Church, even when by the wickedness of men we seem to be expelled from it, as long as we are attached to God, to Jesus Christ, and to the Church herself by charity.
92. To suffer in peace an excommunication and an unjust anathema rather than betray truth, is to imitate St. Paul; far be it from rebelling against authority or of destroying unity.

This end result of the Unigenitus document was more than to condemn the beliefs of the Jansenist Church that had been deemed as heretical by the Rome. It was an instrument used by Rome to establish supremacy of the Pope over the Churches in France and the Netherlands. It is easy to see from the condemnation of beliefs such as those above which had been embraced and taught from the time of the Early Church that the primary goal of the Roman Church was to prevent any questioning of the magisterium of the Church and the Pope.

Furthermore by deeming that acceptance was essential to salvation the foundation was being laid to eliminate the necessity that before doctrine and dogma be binding upon all faithful the Church as a whole must accept the decisions as Truth. Even with the controversy that this document created eventually the Pope, and teachings of the Jesuits, prevailed and the French church sought a new home in the Netherlands in the See of Utrecht.

The Churches of Willibrord - Netherlands

Unfortunately the Church in the Netherlands was facing the same problems as the French church. Not only was the Dutch church resisting accepting the Bull Unigenitus as originally presented but also now there was an insistence that acceptance of Bull in its entirety was necessary to salvation [12]. In addition to this controversy the Jesuits were now teaching everywhere other new and controversial doctrines such as devotion to the Sacred Heart and Immaculate Conception, neither of which had their foundations in the teachings of the Early Church.

The Dutch government itself was Protestant and had no concern or interest in this dispute so the See of Utrecht stood alone against the Jesuits and the Pope.

The schism of the Utrecht See had already begun to form when in 1702, when the Pope deposed the Vicar Apostolic Patras Codde and appointed a new bishop loyal to Rome and the Pope. The result was that many of the clergy and laity of the Catholic Church in Holland remained loyal to Codde. The followers of Codde began to call themselves Roman Catholics of the "Old Episcopal Clergy" (Old Catholics) [7]. This name indicates that they saw themselves as Catholics adhering to the old ways of governing the church as a national Catholic Church.

Over the next few years there were several attempts of reconciliation between the Church in Holland and the Roman Catholic Church. Needless to say none of these attempts were successful and eventually the Church in Holland found themselves without bishops. The pope refused to consecrate a new bishop thinking that this would be the end of the dissenters in the church in Holland.

The Church in Holland entreated the bishop of Babylon to consecrate a Bishop. The Bishop of Babylon agreed and on October 15th, 1724 Cornelius van Steenoven was consecrated the seventh Archbishop of Utrecht. At this point in history the Church of Utrecht had begun her career as a Catholic Church independent of the See of Rome.

The Apex of the Conflict: Power of the Pope - Two New Dogmas

In the mid-19th century Pope Pius IX in retaliation to what the Church perceived as modernism decided as a demonstration of his own fullness of power, and de facto Infallibility, to promulgate a Dogma entirely by himself outside of council. Promulgation of the Dogma had traditionally always been taken at council, and usually in a situation of conflict, as a means to resolve or reject a heresy.

Pope Pius IX had in mind though a Dogma that would further reinforce the Roman system, that Dogma being the Immaculate Conception of Mary. He declared the Immaculate Conception of Dogma in the year 1854.

Often time the Roman Dogma of the Immaculate Conception is confused by uninformed people with the Dogma of Virgin Birth from which it must be carefully distinguished. As we have discussed previously the dogma of the

Virgin Birth is the belief that our Lord was born of a Virgin, which is taught in the Gospels, asserted in the Creeds, and accepted by all orthodox Christians.

> ### More on the Dogma of the Immaculate Conception
>
> *The dogma of the Immaculate Conception is the belief that our Lord's Mother was without sin, original or actual, from the first moment of her existence, which is unknown to Scripture and to the Early Church. It is easy to see though why the Roman Church developed this doctrine since they had adopted belief that that original sin was not merely a defect, but actual guilt due to the act of conception in fallen man, which could not take place without sin. The Latin theologians of the Middle Ages accepted this teaching and some of them argued that our Lord's Mother could not have been separated from Him by guilt even for a moment, and that therefore she must have been excluded by a special Divine privilege from the guilt with which everyone else (except, of course, her Divine Son) is conceived and born.*
>
> *There is no trace of any such teaching in the New Testament. On the contrary, St. Paul says, "All have sinned, and come short of the glory of God" (Rom. 3:16). The Early Church Fathers knew of no such doctrine. They all teach that our Lord alone was without sin. St. John Chrysostom (with other Fathers) even says that Blessed Mary sinned when she interfered at the marriage of Cana so as to deserve rebuke (St. John 2:3). Whatever we may think of his interpretation, it at least shows that he did not know of any belief that the Blessed Virgin was sinless, still less that she was immaculately conceived.*
>
> *As a result of this dogma in the Roman Communion, there are many widely held opinions about the Blessed Virgin; for instance, that as our Lord is the Head of the Church, our Lady is the Neck, so that prayers to Him must go through her (a belief specially commended by Pope Pius X in his letter to the Society of the Rosary); that the Mother of God can command her Divine Son to do her bidding;*
> *that whereas He is the King of justice, she is the Queen of mercy, and is therefore more willing to hear our prayers than He is; and other ideas still more extravagant.* [14]

Needless to say these actions once again caused great controversy within the Roman Church. Over the next few years the controversy was fueled by actions taken by Roman Church under the guidance of the Pope against the perceived threat of "modernism". In order to protect the church Clerical Associations and Bible Societies were condemned, as was the freedom of conscience, religion and the press, along with civil marriage.

In addition an index of books forbidden to Catholics was developed. On this list were the works of Copernicus and Galileo and of philosophers such as Pascal, Spinoza, Descartes, and Kant, to name but a few [13].

The defining moment came on July 18, 1870 when the Roman Church in less than full council declared the Dogma of Papal Infallibility, which states:

1. *That the Pope has a legal binding primacy of jurisdiction over every single national church and every individual Christian.*
2. *The pope possesses the gift of Infallibility and his own solemn magisterial decisions. These solemn (ex cathedra) decisions are Infallible on the basis or special support from all the Holy Spirit and are immutable (irreformable), intrinsically, not by virtue of the ascent of the Church.* [Ibid]

Out of protests to this new Dogma the Church in Germany and other countries in Central Europe separated from the Roman Catholic Church. The leader of this movement was the celebrated Dr Ignatius von Dollinger[8], a Theological Professor of the University of Munich. The new church needed a bishop and clergy and sought out recognition from the Dutch church. The Church in Holland consecrated +Reinkins as first Bishop of the German Old Catholic Church. The Church in Germany was the first to use the name "Old Catholic" in its name. Eventually, under the leadership of the Church of Holland, these Old Catholic communities joined together to form the Utrecht Union of Churches.

European Old Catholic Beliefs

I would now like to provide the two main historical documents that establish both the worship style as well as the theological position of the Old Catholic Churches in Europe. These documents are, *The Fourteen Theses of the Old Catholic Union Conference* written at Bonn in 1874, and *The Declaration of Utrecht* written in 1889.
Without doubt these documents are the cornerstone of the beliefs of Old Catholic Faith. While the original text was in German (not Latin) an English translation follows:

The Fourteen Theses of The Old Catholic Union Conference at Bonn, September 14th – 16th, 1874 [12]

I. We agree that the apocryphal or deutero-canonical books of the Old Testament are not of the same canonicity as the books contained in the Hebrew Canon.

II. We agree that no translation of Holy Scripture can claim an authority superior to that of the original text.

III. We agree that the reading of Holy Scripture in the vulgar tongue cannot be lawfully forbidden.

IV. We agree that, in general, it is more fitting, and in accordance with the spirit of the Church, that the Liturgy should be in the tongue understood by the people.

V. We agree that Faith working by Love, not Faith without Love, is the means and condition of Man's justification before God.

VI. Salvation cannot be merited by "merit of condignity," because there is no proportion between the infinite worth of salvation promised by God and the finite worth of man's works.

VII. We agree that the doctrine of "opera supererogationis" and of a "thesaurus meritorium sanctorum," i.e., that the overflowing merits of the Saints can be transferred to others, either by the rulers of the Church, or by the authors of the good works themselves, is untenable.

VIII. 1. We acknowledge that the number of sacraments was fixed at seven, first in the twelfth century, and then was received into the general teaching of the Church, not as a tradition coming down from the Apostles or from the earliest of times, but as the result of theological speculation.   2. Catholic theologians acknowledge, and we acknowledge with them, that Baptism and the Eucharist are "principalia, praecipus, eximia salutis nostrae sacramenta."

IX. 1. The Holy Scriptures being recognized as the primary rule of Faith, we agree that the genuine tradition, i.e. the unbroken transmission partly oral, partly in writing of the doctrine delivered by Christ and the Apostles is an authoritative source of teaching for all successive generations of Christians. This tradition is partly to be found in the consensus of the great ecclesiastical bodies standing in historical continuity with the primitive Church, partly to be gathered by scientific method from the written documents of all centuries. 2. We acknowledge that the Church of England; and the Churches derived through her, have maintained unbroken the Episcopal succession.

X. We reject the new Roman doctrine of the Immaculate Conception of the Blessed Virgin Mary, as being contrary to the tradition of the first thirteen centuries, according to which Christ alone is conceived without sin.

XI. We agree that the practice of confession of sins before the congregation or a Priest, together with the exercise of the power of the keys, has come down to us from the primitive Church, and that, purged from abuses and free from constraint, it should be preserved in the Church.

XII. We agree that "indulgences" can only refer to penalties actually imposed by the Church herself.

XIII. We acknowledge that the practice of the commemoration of the faithful departed, i.e. the calling down of a richer outpouring of Christ's grace upon them, has come down to us from the primitive Church, and is to be preserved in the Church.

XIV. 1. The Eucharistic celebration in the Church is not a continuous repetition or renewal of the propitiatory sacrifice offered once forever by Christ upon the cross; but its sacrificial character consists in this, that it is the permanent memorial of it, and a representation and presentation on earth of that one oblation of Christ for the salvation of redeemed mankind, which according to the Epistle to the Hebrews (9:11,12), is continuously presented in heaven by Christ, who now appears in the presence of God for us (9:24).
2. While this is the character of the Eucharist in reference to the sacrifice of Christ, it is also a sacred feast, wherein the faithful, receiving the Body and Blood of our Lord, have communion one with another (I Cor. 10:17).

The Declaration of Utrecht, 1889 [12]

We adhere faithfully to the Rule of Faith laid down by St. Vincent of Lerins in these terms: "Id teneamus, quod ubique, quod semper, quod ab omnibus creditum est; hoc est etenim vere proprieque catholicum." *(Hold fast that faith which has been believed everywhere [universally], always, and by all.)* For this reason we preserve in professing the faith of the primitive Church, as formulated in the oecumenical synods and specified precisely by the unanimously accepted decisions of the Oecumenical Councils held in the undivided Church of the first thousand years.

We therefore reject the decrees of the so-called Council of the Vatican, which were promulgated July 18th, 1870, concerning the infallibility and the universal Episcopate of the Bishop of Rome, decrees which are in contradiction with the faith of the ancient Church, and which destroy its ancient canonical constitution by attributing to the Pope the plentitude of ecclesiastical powers over all Dioceses and over all the faithful. By denial of this primatial jurisdiction we do not wish to deny the historical primacy which several Oecumenical Councils and Fathers of the ancient Church have attributed to the Bishop of Rome by recognizing him as the Primus inter pares. *(first among equals)* We also reject the dogma of the Immaculate Conception promulgated by Pius IX in 1854 in defiance of the Holy Scriptures and in contradiction to the tradition of the centuries.

As for other Encyclicals published by the Bishops of Rome in recent times for example, the Bulls Unigenitus and Auctorem fidei, and the Syllabus of 1864, we reject them on all such points as are in contradiction with the doctrine of the primitive Church, and we do not recognize them as binding on the consciences of the faithful. We also renew the ancient protests of the Catholic Church of Holland against the errors of the Roman Curia, and against its attacks upon the rights of national Churches.

We refuse to accept the decrees of the Council of Trent in matters of discipline, and as for the dogmatic decisions of that Council we accept them only so far as they are in harmony with the teaching of the primitive Church.

Considering that the Holy Eucharist has always been the true central point of Catholic worship, we consider it our right to declare that we maintain with perfect fidelity the ancient Catholic doctrine concerning the Sacrament of the Altar, by believing that we receive the Body and Blood of our Saviour Jesus Christ under the species of bread and wine. The Eucharistic celebration in the Church is neither a continual repetition nor a renewal of the expiatory sacrifice which Jesus offered once for all upon the Cross: but it is a sacrifice because it is the perpetual commemoration of the sacrifice offered upon the Cross, and it is the act by which we represent upon earth and appropriate to ourselves the one offering which Jesus Christ makes in Heaven, according to the Epistle to the Hebrews 9:11-12, for the salvation of redeemed humanity, by appearing for us in the presence of God (Heb. 9:24). The character of the Holy Eucharist being thus understood, it is, at the same time, a sacrificial feast, by means of which the faithful in receiving the Body and Blood of our Saviour, enter into communion with one another (I Cor. 10:17).

We hope that Catholic theologians, in maintaining the faith of the undivided Church, will succeed in establishing an agreement upon questions which have been controverted ever since the divisions which arose between the Churches. We exhort the priests under our jurisdiction to teach, both by preaching and by the instruction of the young, especially the essential Christian truths professed by all the Christian confessions, to avoid, in discussing controverted doctrines, any violation of truth or charity, and in word and deed to set an example to the members.

By maintaining and professing faithfully the doctrine of Jesus Christ, by refusing to admit those errors which by the fault of men have crept into the Catholic Church, by laying aside the abuses in ecclesiastical matters, together with the worldly tendencies of the hierarchy, we believe that we shall be able to combat efficaciously the great evils of our day, which are unbelief and indifference in matters of religion.

Utrecht, 24th September 1889 - +Heykamp- +Rinkel - +Diependaal - +Reinkens -+Herzog'

By careful reading of the these two documents it is fairly easy to develop the following outline of the basic beliefs of the European Churches:

- Profess and accept the faith as set forth by the Early Church and specifically the Ecumenical Councils of the undivided Church (of which there were seven).
- Rejection of Papal Infallibility.
- Do not accept the Roman Catholic Dogma of the Immaculate Conception of Mary, and therefore the subsequent Dogma of the Assumption of Mary.
- Refuse to accept the Dogmas and Decrees of the Council of Trent, unless such doctrine is in agreement with the declarations of the first seven ecumenical councils.
- Believe in real presence and seven sacraments and in the understanding of the meaning of "sacrifice" as did the Early Church and not as the Roman Church teaches.
- Priests are directed to teach and profess a faith that is believed and held common by all "Catholics".
- Rejection of the deutero-canonical books as part of the Canon of the Bible.

- The Bible should be translated into the language of the people.
- Liturgy in the "tongue of the people".
- Confession may be before priest or congregation.
- Commemoration of the departed in a valid tradition from the primitive church.
- Salvation not possible by "works".
- Scriptures are primary rule of Faith – agree that unbroken "genuine tradition" source of teaching

In closing this section Hans Kung in his the book *The Catholic Church*, has this to say about the Old Catholic Church:

This is a church which continues to be Catholic but is Rome-free. With validly consecrated bishops, it seeks to hold firm to the faith of the church of the first millennium (the first seven councils), to implement a synodical episcopal constitution with great autonomy for the local church, and accord the pope no more than a primacy of honor. Customs introduced in the middle ages, or only in the nineteenth century, like compulsory celibacy, the obligation to go to confession once per year, the cult of relics, the rosary, veneration of the heart of Jesus and the heart of Mary are all repudiated. In many respects this little bold and ecumenically open Old Catholic Church from the beginning anticipated the reforms of the Second Vatican Council and recently has even gone beyond them with the ordination of women. (13 - page 167)

Section IV
Old Catholicism Comes to the New World

Independent Movement Today

If you do an Internet Search for "Old Catholic", odds are the search engine will provide you with links to numerous sites. As you begin to explore these sites you will find all sorts of information concerning the Old Catholic Faith. You will find numerous denominations, parishes, seminaries, histories, theologies, and ideologies. And you will soon begin to learn that an "Autocephalous" Bishop heads each of these small independent churches up. You will very quickly discover that the beliefs, teachings, histories, and theologies vary radically from group to group and sometimes within a group!

For example some of these "Old Catholic Communions" are ultra conservative and profess a Latin Rite, Celibacy, Holy Orders for men only, and closed communion. At other "Old Catholic" sites you will read how the mass is said in the vernacular, open communion is touted as the norm, auricular confession is not required for remission of sins, and both men and women may serve as clergy. There are also those that claim to be "Old Catholic you must reject the Roman Dogmas of Infallibility and the Immaculate Conception and then they are others who accept these dogmas and will claim that the reason that they are not in communion with Rome is that the current Pope is not really "THE" Pope. You might read at one site how Old Catholics consider homosexuality to be a sin, and only a mouse click later find "Old Catholics" that cater to the "Gay" community.

As you continue your search, you will discover that there are about as many different "Old Roman Catholics", "Old Catholics", and "Independent Catholics" as there are protestant denominations. In addition, as for beliefs and histories, it could be likened to an ice cream parlor with, "a flavor for every one". In all likelihood, you will become increasingly confused in your attempt to discern and might very well just give up your quest.

Apostolic Succession

The Independent and Old Catholic movement in the Americas retains valid apostolic lines from several different Sees.
These include the Old Catholic Churches of Europe, The Roman Church, The Orthodox Churches, and the Anglican Church. However you will find that more often than not the names of two particular bishops seems to surface as being instrumental in the spread of Old Catholicism to the "New World". These two are, Bishop Arnold Harris Matthew and Bishop Joseph René Vilatte. Below is a brief history of these two bishops. For a more

detailed history I recommend that reading *The Old Catholic Church A history and Chronology 2nd Edition* by Bishop Karl Pruter. (14)

Bishop Arnold Harris Mathew

Arnold Mathew was formerly a Roman Catholic Priest who became disgruntled with the Roman Church. Then Fr. Mathew opened a dialog wit the Swiss Old Catholic prelate, Bishop Eduard Herzog concerning the development of the Old Catholic church in Great Britain. He was elected as bishop and was consecrated by Geraldus Gul, Old Catholic Archbishop of Utrecht, in the year1908 (Ibid).

Unfortunately Bishop Mathew had underestimated the potential for acceptance of Old Catholicism in Great Britain and the church did not grow. Eventually he withdrew from union with the church at Utrecht. Even though Bishop Mathews vision of Old Catholicism in Great Britain was not to be realized he was instrumental in the Old Catholic movement in that he consecrated Prince de Landas Berghes et de Rache and Frederick Samuel Willoughby. These two bishops would be instrumental in the development of Old Catholicism in the Americas, especially Bishop de Landas Berghes et de Rache who in the year 1916 consecrated Carmel Henry Carfora (Ibid). *(This is the principle line of succession for the OCCNA.)*

Bishop Joseph Rene' Vilatte

Joseph René Vilatte is often credited with being the first person to bring Old Catholicism to North America. A child of French immigrants he was raised in Montreal. Vilatte, who became a Presbyterian missionary in Wisconsin, found that not many of the Belgians desired to become Presbyterian. In an attempt to gain more members, and with the help of the Anglicans, Vilatte was ordained in the Old Catholic union by Bishop Herzog of Switzerland in 1885.

While Vilatte had been ordained an Old Catholic priest he ended up serving Episcopal churches were he established the mission Church of the Precious Blood in Little Sturgeon. He later established a second mission in Green Bay, the Church of the Blessed Sacrament, which eventually became an Episcopal Church. He was never consecrated a bishop in the Old Catholic churches instead he was consecrated by Mar Julius I, bishop of the Independent Catholic Church of Ceylon, Goa, India to be the Old Catholic Bishop of America. (Ibid)

Relations With Utrecht

The German Old Catholic Church states on its website[9] that the Bishops Matthew and Vilatte were consecrated under false pretenses and therefore their orders should be considered invalid. In essence they state that just as a Church cannot be without a Bishop – a Bishop cannot be without a Church.

It is ironic that the German Church is taking an identical stance against the Old Catholics in this country as the Roman Church took against them. (The Roman Church declared the consecrations of the Old Catholic bishops as invalid even though the Independent See of Utrecht performed them.) The invalidation claim seems particularly inappropriate since Bishop Vilatte who was not even consecrated by the German Church and Bishop Arnold Harris Mathew assisted Archbishop Gerardus Gul, of Utrecht in the consecration of Johann Michael Kowalski, which meant that his consecration was certainly considered valid at this time. How sad it is that they [European Old Catholics] have become entangled in the very system they wished to leave.

Common traits of the Churches I found.

Many on these small independent communions that claim to be Old Catholic devote a lot of time and energy to defending their apostolic succession, attempting to be old (in age), and defending their "valid orders" against Rome and each other. I have learned that many of the churches that call themselves "Old Catholic" are really only "Old Catholic" in the sense that they trace their apostolic lines through the Episcopacy of the European Churches. None of the Independent or Old Catholic Churches in the United Sates that I am aware of are in communion with the Roman or the Old Catholic Churches of Europe (with the exception of the Polish National Catholic Church).

Many of these small independent communions work very hard to justify their particular "flavor" of Christianity. They are not concerned how their theological perspective compares to other each other, to the Old Catholic Churches in Europe, to the beliefs and theology of the original founders of the denomination, or in some cases even to the councils and dogmas of the Early Church. Many have more clergy that laity. Many consist of a sole Bishop. Many have no laity or ministry only an Internet site to use as a pulpit.

After many days of searching, study, and research I now classify Catholic Churches that are not in communion with Rome into three basic groups – they are: Independent, Old Roman Catholic, and Old Catholic. I have also noticed certain similarities in the structure and theology of each group. A brief synopsis of each group follows:

Old Roman Catholic

These Churches are usually pre Vatican II in both their worship and theology. Most prefer to use a traditional rite; some use the Tridentine Latin Mass. Many stress (or require), celibacy, ordain men only, and may require auricular confession before a priest. There is a tendency to emphasize form (e.g., only receive communion on the tongue) and Church authority (rigid control by the bishop). In short, for the most part this group is pre-Vatican II Roman Catholics who tend to focus on the doctrines and dogmas of the council of Trent and the First Vatican Council.

Independent Catholic

While it is my opinion that all Catholic Churches not in communion with Rome are in fact "Independent Catholic" I chose to apply this title to those individuals, and groups, that basically agree with the teachings of the present day Roman Church (Vatican II). In this group you will find that many of the Clergy would in fact be Roman if could they could. Often these churches are formed by those who in order to fulfill a call to vocation had to leave Rome because they were married, female, etc.

Quite often those in this category will refer to themselves as "Old Catholic" yet they readily accept Dogmas like the Immaculate Conception and Assumption of Mary, which as we know were rejected by the Old Catholic Churches.

Also, it will be found that some of these Churches were formed as their founder's beliefs and theology has been rejected by Rome or other mainstream catholic denominations. (Such as allowing and blessing homosexual marriages and clergy, embracing new age theology, etc.)

Old Catholics

The Polish National Catholic Church was the only U.S. Church recognized by the European Churches and was a member of the Union of Utrecht. It should also be mentioned that The Philippine Independent Catholic Church (which is the largest of the Old Catholic Churches with over one million members, and a member of the Utrecht Union is starting to establish a presence in North America as well.)

This is not to say that there are not any other Old Catholic Churches in the Americas for there are many. In fact, there are many independent jurisdictions that adhere to the doctrines and beliefs as established by the Utrecht Union. Due to the number involved and the tendency for new churches to be established quickly I will not attempt to name them. Instead I offer that the reader, by now understanding the core beliefs of Old Catholicism should be better equipped to discern these jurisdictions when seeking to locate an Old Catholic Parish.

Section V
The Old Catholic Church of North America

What about the OCCNA? How does its beliefs compare to our understating of Old Catholicism as we now understand it? Below you will find the Statements of Belief as established by the House of Bishops of the OCCNA. After taking time to compare these beliefs to the Declaration of Utrecht and the Fourteen Thesis of the Old Catholic Conference at Bonn I think it will be obvious that the OCCNA is indeed an Old Catholic Church. You will notice that some of the beliefs serve to define specific doctrine of the OCCNA in matters such as marriage, new age theology, abortion, ordinations of women, etc.

Beliefs of the OCCNA

1. We believe that Jesus is the Christ and our personal savior.
2. We believe in The Holy Trinity.
3. We believe in the Nicene Creed.
4. We believe in the inerrancy and divine inspiration of Holy Scriptures.
5. We believe in the seven sacraments of the Church: Baptism, Confirmation, Holy Eucharist, Anointing of the Sick (Extreme Unction), Reconciliation (Confession and Absolution), Marriage, and Holy Orders.
6. We believe in the **Real Presence of Jesus Christ in the Eucharist** as set forth by the Declaration of Utrecht and Canons of OCCNA.
7. We believe that all Holy Orders (bishops, priests, and deacons) are open to both men and women.
8. We believe that celibacy of those in Holy Orders is a personal decision.
9. We believe and hold apostolic succession.
10. We believe and accept the doctrines of the Seven Early Church Ecumenical Councils.
11. We believe and appreciate the wisdom and guidance of the Early Church Fathers.
12. We appreciate the wisdom and guidance of the founding Fathers of the Old Catholic Movement as expressed in historic documents of the Old Catholic Churches of Europe particularly the Declaration of Utrecht and The Fourteen Theses of the Old Catholic Church at Bonn.
13. We do not ordain homosexuals to ministry nor perform same-sex marriages.
14. We believe that abortion and euthanasia is the taking of human life.
15. We believe in the responsible stewardship of our planet.
16. We believe in One Holy Catholic and Apostolic Church.

17. We believe in the sanctity of marriage, however we believe that Jesus is merciful and those who have been divorced and/or remarried are offered the sacraments of the church.
18. We believe that family planning is a personal decision between a husband and wife.
19. We believe and follow scripture in all matters.
20. We believe in the scriptural teaching of Jesus Christ.

Liturgy of the OCCNA

The following statements concerning Liturgy are excerpted from the Canons of the IOOCA.:

   A. *The matter and form of Sacraments will be identical in intent and form to those used by other historic Catholic churches, specifically the Roman Catholic Church, the Episcopal, Anglican, Old Catholic and Eastern Orthodox Churches and in compliance with the "Essentials of a Catholic Eucharist" as promulgated by the College of Bishops.*

   B. *Rituals surrounding the matter and form of the Sacraments will show respect for the Catholic liturgical traditions, but may reflect local customs.*

   C. *In the liturgy references to the Trinity are in the traditional Catholic format.*

From these statements one is able to determine that the House of Bishops offers the local parish a wide degree of flexibility to establish a worship style that is familiar to all that attend. This is why you might find one parish using the Episcopal Book of Common Prayer, another using a modified Roman Rite, and yet another using a rite that is a combination of European Old Catholic, Anglican, and Orthodox. Regardless of which rite is used there are certain essential elements of the Mass that the House of Bishops has set forth in the Canons. As in the Early Church each local parish / diocese is catholic in that the fullness of Christ is manifested both in and through it and the OCCNA is part of the universal church by accepting intercommunion and concelebration between its dioceses and in accepting all baptized faithful at the altar.

Frequently Asked Questions About the OCCNA

I am divorced and remarried may I receive Communion? Yes. While the OCCNA looks upon matrimony as a sacrament, and believes that marriage should be a lifelong commitment between a man and a woman we do realize though that situations will arise that will lead to divorce.

It is our opinion that to refuse Communion to a divorced individual who is sincerely seeking to repent and turn to Christ is to inflict additional emotional pain and suffering.

Do I have to go to confession? If you are asking if you must confess and repent of your sins to be forgiven – then the answer is yes. If you are asking must you confess your sins before a priest to be forgiven then the answer is no. The OCCNA teaches that the sacrament of Reconciliation is provided in both the General Confession and Absolution, which is included in the Mass, and through private confession to either a Priest or Bishop. It is our belief that the INTENT (sincerity) of the individual takes precedent over form.

What does the OCCNA teach about abortion? The OCCNA considers abortion at any time during the pregnancy to be the taking of a life. We encourage any woman faced with an unwanted pregnancy to consider adoption over abortion. We realize that a woman might be faced with making a decision about a pregnancy that could result in harm, or even loss of life, to herself. In these situations we encourage that she consult with qualified professionals and clergy prior to making her decision. The OCCNA will never turn away a woman who has had an abortion from the loving embrace of Jesus

Since you are not under the authority of the Pope then who is the head of the OCCNA? Jesus Christ is the head of the Church. However, the OCCNA parishes and clergy, like all other Catholic Communions, are under the guidance and authority of a Bishop. The OCCNA maintains valid lines of Apostolic Succession, which can be traced to the ancient and undivided church. All clergy in the OCCNA are ordained by the "laying on of hands".

May Roman Catholics, Episcopalians, Orthodox, or any other denomination receive the sacraments from an OCCNA church/clergy member? Absolutely! The OCCNA encourages faithful from other traditions and denominations to visit our churches and learn more about us. We do not restrict the reception of any sacraments based solely on denomination or tradition.

My spouse is not Catholic may they receive Eucharist/Communion? It is the stance of the OCCNA that all Christians baptized in the Name of the Father, Son, and Holy Spirit are indeed members incorporate in the Body of Christ and should be allowed to fully participate in both the Liturgy and Sacraments of the Church. We believe that our practice of an "open communion" serves to bring those who have fallen away from the Church back to unity in the "Universal" Church in accordance with the teachings of the Holy Fathers. We think it unfortunate that even within those churches that comprise the Catholic Faith that barriers have been established to exclude others from the sacraments and prayer that the Holy Spirit guide all back to the Universal Faith.

What about Pre-Marital Sex?
The OCCNA as well as the Catholic faith holds to the biblical teaching that sexual intercourse is reserved for marriage. Sex is a gift of God to be fully enjoyed and experienced only within marriage. The marriage bed is to be kept "pure and undefiled" (Hebrew 13:4), and men and women are called to remain celibate outside of marriage. Our sexuality, like many other things about us human beings, affects our relationship with God, others, and ourselves. It may be employed as a means of glorifying God and fulfilling His image in us, or it may be perverted and abused as an instrument of sin, causing great damage to others and us. St. Paul writes, "Do you know that your body is the temple of the Holy Spirit who is in you, whom you have from God, and you are not your own? For you were bought at a price; therefore glorify God in your body" (I Corinthians 6:19, 20).

A Short Summary of the Faith[10]

God
God the Father is the fountainhead of the Holy Trinity. The Scriptures reveal the one God is Three Persons - Father, Son, and Holy Spirit - eternally sharing the one divine nature. From the Father the Son is begotten before all ages and all time (Psalm 2:7; II Corinthians 11:31). It is from the Father that the Holy Spirit eternally proceeds (John 15:26). God the Father created all things through the Son, in the Holy Spirit (Genesis 1 and 2; John 1:3; Job 33:4), and we are called to worship Him (John 4:23). The Father loves us and sent His Son to give us everlasting life (John 3:16).

Jesus Christ
Jesus Christ is the Second Person of the Holy Trinity, eternally born of the Father. He became man, and thus He is at once fully God and fully man. The prophets foretold his coming to earth in the Old Testament. Because Jesus Christ is at the heart of Christianity, the Catholic Church has given more attention to knowing Him than to anything or anyone else.

In reciting the Nicene Creed, Catholic Christians regularly affirm the historic faith concerning Jesus as they say, "I believe... in one Lord Jesus Christ, the Son of God, the only begotten, begotten of the Father before all ages, Light of Light, true God of true God; begotten, not made; of one essence with the Father; by Whom all things were made; Who for us men and for our salvation came down from heaven, and was incarnate of the Holy Spirit and the Virgin Mary, and was made man; and was crucified also for us under Pontius Pilate, and suffered and was buried; and the third day He rose again according to the Scriptures; and ascended into heaven, and sits at the right hand of the Father; and He shall come again with glory to judge the living and the dead; Whose kingdom shall have no end."

Incarnation refers to Jesus Christ coming "in the flesh." The eternal Son of God the Father assumed to Himself a complete human nature from the Virgin Mary. He was and is one divine Person, fully possessing from God the Father the entirety of the divine nature, and in His coming in the flesh fully possessing a human nature from the Virgin Mary. By His Incarnation, the Son forever possesses two natures in His one Person. The Son of God, limitless in His divine nature, voluntarily and willingly accepted limitation in His humanity in which He experienced hunger, thirst, fatigue - and ultimately, death. The Incarnation is indispensable to Christianity - there is no Christianity without it. The Scriptures record, "Every spirit that does not confess that Jesus Christ has come in the flesh is not of God" (I John 4:3). By His Incarnation, the Son of God redeemed human nature, a redemption made accessible to all who are joined to Him in His glorified humanity.

The Holy Spirit
The Holy Spirit is one of the Persons of the Holy Trinity and is one in essence with the Father.
He is called the "promise of the Father" (Acts 1:4), given by Christ as a gift to the Church, to empower the Church for service to God (Acts 1:8), to place God's love in our hearts (Romans 5:5), and to impart spiritual gifts (I Corinthians 12:7-13) and virtues (Galatians 5:22, 23) for Christian life and witness.
Catholic Christians believe the biblical promise that the Holy Spirit is given through Chrismation (anointing) at baptism (Acts 2:38). We are to grow in our experience of the Holy Spirit for the rest of our lives.

Sin
Sin literally means to "miss the mark." As St. Paul writes, "All have sinned and fall short of the glory of God" (Romans 3:23). We sin when we pervert what God has given us as good, falling short of His purposes for us. Our sins separate us from God (Isaiah 59:1, 2), leaving us spiritually dead (Ephesians 2:1). To save us, the Son of God assumed our humanity, and being without sin "He condemned sin in the flesh" (Romans 8:3). In His mercy, God forgives our sins when we confess them and turn from them, giving us strength to overcome sin in our lives. "If we confess our sins, He is faithful and just to forgive our sins and to cleanse us from all unrighteousness" (I John 1:9).

Salvation
Salvation is the divine gift through which men and women are delivered from sin and death, united to Christ, and brought into His eternal kingdom. Those who heard St. Peter's sermon on the day of Pentecost asked what they must do to be saved. He answered, "Repent, and let every one of you be baptized in the name of Jesus Christ for the remission of sins; and you shall receive the gift of the Holy Spirit" (Acts 2:38). Salvation begins with these three steps: 1) repent, 2) be baptized, and 3) receive the gift of the Holy Spirit. To repent means to change our mind about how we have been, to turn from our sin and to commit ourselves to Christ. To be baptized means to be born again by being joined into union with Christ. And to receive the gift of the Holy Spirit means to receive the Spirit Who empowers us to enter a new life in Christ, to be nurtured in the Church, and to be conformed to God's image.

Salvation demands faith in Jesus Christ. People cannot save themselves by their own good works. Salvation is "faith working through love." It is an ongoing, life-long process. Salvation is past tense in that, through the death and Resurrection of Christ, we have been saved.
It is present tense, for we are "being saved" by our active participation through faith in our union with Christ by the power of the Holy Spirit. Salvation is also future, for we must yet be saved at His glorious Second Coming.

Baptism
Baptism is the way in which a person is actually united to Christ. The experience of salvation is initiated in the waters of baptism. The Apostle Paul teaches in Romans 6:1-6 that in baptism we experience Christ's death and

resurrection. In it our sins are truly forgiven and we are energized by our union with Christ to live a holy life. Currently, some consider baptism to be only an "outward sign" of belief in Christ. This innovation has no historical or biblical precedent. Others reduce it to a mere perfunctory obedience to Christ's command (cf. Matthew 28:19-20). Still others, ignoring the Bible completely, reject baptism as a vital factor in salvation. The Catholic Faith maintains that these contemporary innovations rob sincere people of the most important assurances that baptism provides - namely that they have been united to Christ and are part of His Church.

New Birth

New Birth is receipt of new life. It is how we gain entrance into God's kingdom and His Church. Jesus said, "Unless one is born of water and the Spirit, he cannot enter the kingdom of God" (John 3:5). From its beginning, the Church has taught that the water is the baptismal water and the Spirit is the Holy Spirit. The new birth occurs in baptism where we die with Christ, are buried with Him, and are raised with Him in the newness of His resurrection, being joined into union with Him in His glorified humanity (Acts 2:38; Romans 6:3-4). The idea that being "born again" is a religious experience disassociated from baptism is a recent one and has no biblical basis whatsoever.

Justification

Justification is a word used in the Scriptures to mean that in Christ we are forgiven and actually made righteous in our living. Justification is not a once-for-all, instantaneous pronouncement guaranteeing eternal salvation, regardless of how wickedly a person might live from that point on. Neither is it merely a legal declaration that an unrighteous person is righteous. Rather, justification is a living, dynamic, day-to-day reality for the one who follows Christ. The Christian actively pursues a righteous life in the grace and power of God granted to all who continue to believe in Him.

Sanctification

Sanctification is being set apart for God. It involves us in the process of being cleansed and made holy by Christ in the Holy Spirit. We are called to be saints and to grow into the likeness of God.
Having been given the gift of the Holy Spirit, we actively participate in sanctification. We cooperate with God, we work together with Him, that we may know Him, becoming by grace what He is by nature.

The Bible

The Bible is the divinely inspired Word of God (II Timothy 3:16), and is a crucial part of God's self-revelation to the human race. The Old Testament tells the history of that revelation from Creation through the Age of the Prophets. The New Testament records the birth and life of Jesus as well as the writings of His Apostles. It also includes some of the history of the early Church and especially sets forth the Church's apostolic doctrine. Though these writings were read in the Churches from the time they first appeared, the earliest listings of all the New Testament books exactly as we know them today is found in the 33rd Canon of a local council held at Carthage in 318, and in a fragment of St. Athanasius of Alexandria's Festal Letter in 367. Both sources list all of the books of the New Testament without exception. A local council, probably held at Rome in 382, set forth a complete list of the canonical books of both the Old and the New Testaments. The Scriptures are at the very heart of Catholic worship and devotion.

Worship

Worship is the rendering of praise, glory, and thanksgiving to God: the Father, the Son, and the Holy Spirit. All humanity is called to worship God. Worship is more than being in the "great-out-of-doors," or listening to a sermon, or singing a hymn. God can be known in His creation, but that does not constitute worship. As helpful as sermons may be, they can never offer a proper substitute for worship. Most prominent in Catholic worship is the corporate praise, thanksgiving, and glory given to God by the Church. This worship is consummated in intimate communion with God at His Holy Table. In worship we touch and experience His eternal kingdom, the age to come, and we join in adoration with the heavenly hosts. We experience the glory of fulfillment of all things in Christ, as truly all in all.

Liturgy

Liturgy is a term used to describe the shape or form of the Church's corporate worship of God. The word "liturgy" derives from a Greek word that means "the common work." All the biblical references to worship in heaven involve liturgy.

In the Old Testament, God ordered a liturgy, or specific pattern of worship. We find it described in detail in the books of Exodus and Leviticus. In the New Testament we find the Church carrying over the worship of Old Testament Israel as expressed in both the synagogue and the temple, adjusting them in keeping with their fulfillment in Christ. The Catholic Liturgy, which developed over many centuries, still maintains that ancient shape of worship.

The main elements in the Liturgy include hymns, the reading and proclamation of the Gospel, prayers, and the Eucharist itself. For Catholic Christians, the expressions "The Liturgy" or "Divine Liturgy" refer to the eucharistic rite instituted by Christ Himself at the Last (Mystical) Supper.

Eucharist

Eucharist literally means "thanksgiving" and early became a synonym for Holy Communion. The Eucharist is the center of worship in the Catholic Church. Because Jesus said of the bread and wine at the Last Supper, "This is my body," "This is my blood," and "Do this in remembrance of Me" (Luke 22:19-20), His followers believe - and do - nothing less. In the Eucharist, we partake mystically of Christ's Body and Blood, which impart His life and strength to us. The celebration of the Eucharist was a regular part of the Church's life from its beginning. Early Christians began calling the Eucharist "the medicine of immortality" because they recognized the great grace of God that was received in it.

Communion of Saints

When Christians depart this life, they remain a vital part of the Church, the body of Christ. They are alive in the Lord and "registered in heaven" (Hebrews 12:23). They worship God (Revelation 4:10) and inhabit His heavenly dwelling places (John 14:2). In the Eucharist we come "to the city of the living God" and join in communion with the saints in our worship of God (Hebrews 12:22). They are that "great cloud of witnesses" which surrounds us, and we seek to imitate them in running "the race set before us" (Hebrews 12:1). Rejecting or ignoring the communion of saints is a denial of the fact that those who have died in Christ are still part of his holy Church.

Confession

Confession is the open admission of known sins before God and man. It means literally "to agree with" God concerning our sins.

St. James the Apostle admonishes us to confess our sins to God before the elders, or priests, as they are called today (James 5:16). We are also exhorted to confess our sins directly to God (I John 1:9).
The Old Catholic Church follows the New Testament practices of confession before a priest as well as private confession to the Lord. Confession is one of the most significant means of repenting, and receiving assurance that even our worst sins are truly forgiven. It is also one of our most powerful aids to forsaking and overcoming those sins.

Mary

Mary is called Theotokos, meaning "God-bearer" or "the Mother of God," because she bore the Son of God in her womb and from her He took His humanity. Elizabeth, the mother of John the Baptist, recognized this reality when she called Mary, "the Mother of my Lord" (Luke 1:43). Mary said of herself, "All generations shall call me blessed" (Luke 1:48). So we, Catholic, in our generation, call her blessed. Mary lived a chaste and holy life, and we honor her highly as the model of holiness, the first of the redeemed, the Mother of the new humanity in her Son.

Prayer To The Saints
The Catholic Church accepts Prayer To The Saints, why? Because physical death is not a defeat for a Christian. It is a glorious passage into heaven. The Christian does not cease to be a part of the Church at death. God forbid! Nor is he set aside, idle until the Day of Judgment. The True Church is composed of all who are in Christ - in heaven and on earth. It is not limited in membership to those presently alive. Those in heaven with Christ are alive, in communion with God, worshipping God, doing their part in the body of Christ. They actively pray to God for all those in the Church - and perhaps, indeed, for the whole world (Ephesians 6:8; Revelation 8:3). So we pray to the saints who have departed this life, seeking their prayers, even as we ask Christian friends on earth to pray for us.

Apostolic Succession
Apostolic Succession has been a watershed issue since the second century, not as a mere dogma, but as crucial to the preservation of the faith. Certain false teachers would appear, insisting they were authoritative representatives of the Christian Church. Claiming authority from God by appealing to special revelations, some were even inventing lineages of teachers supposedly going back to Christ or the Apostles. In response, the early Church insisted there was an authoritative apostolic succession passed down from generation to generation.

They recorded that actual lineage, showing how its clergy were ordained by those chosen by the successors of the Apostles chosen by Christ Himself. Apostolic succession is an indispensable factor in preserving Church unity. Those in the succession are accountable to it, and are responsible to ensure all teaching and practice in the Church is in keeping with Her apostolic foundations. Mere personal conviction that one's teaching is correct can never be considered adequate proof of accuracy. Today, critics of apostolic succession are those who stand outside that historic succession and seek a self-identity with the early Church only. The burgeoning number of denominations in the world can be accounted for in large measure by a rejection of apostolic succession.

Councils of the Church
A monumental conflict (recorded in Acts 15) arose in the early Church over legalism, the keeping of Jewish laws by the Christians, as means of salvation. "So the apostles and elders came together [in council] to consider the matter" (Acts 15:6). This council, held in Jerusalem, set the pattern for the subsequent calling of councils to settle problems. There have been hundreds of such councils - local and regional - over the centuries of the history of the Church, and seven councils specifically designated Ecumenical, that is, considered to apply to the whole Church. Aware that God has spoken through the Ecumenical Councils, the Old Catholic Church looks particularly to them for authoritative teaching about the faith and practice of the Church.

Creed
Creed comes from the Latin credo, "I believe." From the earliest days of the Church, creeds have been living confessions of what Christians believe and not simply formal, academic, Church pronouncements. Such confessions of faith appear as early as the New Testament, where, for example, St. Paul quotes a creed to remind Timothy, "God...was revealed in the flesh" (I Timothy 3:16). The creeds were approved by Church councils, usually to give a concise statement of the truth in the face of the invasion of heresy.

The most important creed in Christendom is the Nicene Creed, the product of two Ecumenical Councils in the fourth century. Delineated in the midst of a life-and-death controversy, it contains the essence of New Testament teaching about the Holy Trinity, guarding that life-giving truth against those who would change the very nature of God and reduce Jesus Christ to a created being, rather than God in the flesh.

The creeds give us a sure interpretation of the Scriptures against those who would distort them to support their own religious schemes. Called the "symbol of faith" and confessed in many of the services of the Church, the Nicene Creed constantly reminds the Catholic Christian of what he personally believes, keeping his faith on track.

Spiritual Gifts

When the young Church was getting under way, God poured out His Holy Spirit upon the Apostles and their followers, giving them spiritual gifts to build up the Church and to serve each other. Among the specific gifts of the Spirit mentioned in the New Testament are: apostleship, prophecy, evangelism, pastoring, teaching, healing, helps, administrations, knowledge, wisdom, tongues, interpretation of tongues. These and other spiritual gifts are recognized in the Old Catholic Church. The need for them varies with the times. The gifts of the Spirit are most in evidence in the liturgical and sacramental life of the Church.

Second Coming

Amid the current speculation in some corners of Christendom surrounding the Second Coming of Christ and how it may come to pass, it is comforting to know that the beliefs of the Catholic Church are basic. Catholic Christians confess with conviction that Jesus Christ "will come again to judge the living and the dead," and that His "kingdom will have no end." Catholic preaching does not attempt to predict God's prophetic schedule, but to encourage Christian people to have their lives in order so that they might be confident before Him when He comes (I John 2:28).

Heaven

Heaven is the place of God's throne, beyond time and space. It is the abode of God's angels, as well as of the saints who have passed from this life. We pray, "Our Father, who art in heaven."
Though Christians live in this world, they belong to the kingdom of heaven, and that kingdom is their true home. However, heaven is not only for the future. Neither is it some distant place billions of light years away in a nebulous "great beyond." For the Catholic, heaven is part of Christian life and worship. The Eucharist is heavenly worship, heaven on earth. St. Paul teaches that we are raised up with Christ in heavenly places (Ephesians 2:6), "fellow citizens with the saints and members of the household of God" (Ephesians 2:19). At the end of the age, a new heaven and a new earth will be revealed (Revelation 21:1).

Hell

Hell, unpopular as it is to modern people, is real. The Catholic Church understands hell as a place of eternal torment for those who willfully reject the grace of God. Our Lord once said, "If your hand makes you sin, cut it off. It is better for you to enter into life maimed, than having two hands, to go to hell, into the fire that never shall be quenched - where their worm does not die, and the fire is not quenched" (Mark 9:44-45). He challenged the religious hypocrites with the question: "How can you escape the condemnation of hell?" (Matthew 23:33). His answer is, "God did not send His Son into the world to condemn the world, but that the world through Him might be saved" (John 3:17). There is a day of judgment coming, and there is a place of punishment for those who have hardened their hearts against God. It does make a difference how we will live this life. Those who of their own free will reject the grace and mercy of God must forever bear the consequences of that choice.

Creation:

Catholic Christians confess God as Creator of heaven and earth (Genesis 1:1, the Nicene Creed). Creation did not just come into existence by itself. God made it all. "By faith we understand that the worlds were framed by the word of God" (Hebrews 11:3). Catholic Christians do not believe the Bible to be a science textbook on creation, as some mistakenly maintain, but rather to be God's revelation of Himself and His salvation. Also, we do not view science textbooks, helpful though they may be, as God's revelation. They may contain both known facts and speculative theory, but they are not infallible. Catholic Christians refuse to build an unnecessary and artificial wall between science and the Christian faith. Rather, they understand honest scientific investigation as a potential encouragement to faith, for all truth is from God.

Bibliography

References Cited:
1. New Advent Catholic Encyclopedia (http://www.newadvent.org/)
2. I Clement in *The Early Church Fathers* (Nashville, TN. Broadman Press, 1980
3. First Apology I: 65
4. To The Philadelphians 4
5. *Cyprian* (c.50, W). 5.374,35 and 5.377
6. *The Encarta® Desk Encyclopedia* Copyright © 1998 Microsoft Corporation. All rights reserved.
7. *The Old Catholic Parish Church of St. Peter and St. Paul Parish in Rotterdam* (http://www.paradijskerk.nl/engels.html)
8. *The Encyclopedia Britannica*
9. *OC Church of Germany* – http://www.alt-katholiken.de/index-e.html
10. Adapted from the Russian Orthodox Church - http://www.orre/catech
11. Bishop. Karl Pruter, *The Old Catholic Church A history and Chronology 2nd Edition*, (San Bernardino, CA., St. Willibrord's Press, 1996)
12. Rev. C. B. Moss, *The Old Catholic Movement Its History and Origins 2nd Edition*, (Eureka Springs, AR., The Episcopal Book Club, 1977) Note: This book is out of print.
13. Hans Kung, *The Catholic Church A Short History*, (New York, NY. Random House Publishing, 2001)
14. Rev. C. B. Moss, *The Christian Faith: An Introduction to Dogmatic Theology*, (New York, BY. Morehouse-Gorham Co., Society For Promoting Christian Knowledge, 1943)

Texts Used and Recommended Reading
I. Bishop. Karl Pruter, *The Old Catholic Church A history and Chronology 2nd Edition*, (San Bernardino, CA., St. Willibrord's Press, 1996)
II. Hans Kung, *The Catholic Church A Short History*, (New York, NY. Random House Publishing, 2001)
III. Rev. C. B. Moss, *The Old Catholic Movement Its History and Origins 2nd Edition*, (Eureka Springs, AR., The Episcopal Book Club, 1977) Note: This book is out of print.
IV. Rev. C. B. Moss, *The Christian Faith: An Introduction to Dogmatic Theology*, (New York, BY. Morehouse-Gorham Co., Society For Promoting Christian Knowledge, 1943) NOTE: This book is out of print however it may be found online at (http://justus.anglican.org/resources/pc/cbmoss/)
V. Bishop, Kallistos Ware, *The Orthodox Way*, (Crestwood, NY., St. Vladimir's Seminary Press, 2002)
VI. Clark Carlton, *The Truth What Every Roman Catholic Should Know About the Orthodox Faith*, (Salisbury, MA., Regina Orthodox Press, 1999)
VII. Fr. Michael Pomazansky, *Orthodox Dogmatic Theology A Concise Exposition 2nd Edition*, (Jordanville, NY., Holy Trinity Monastery, 1997)
VIII. Leo Donald Davis, *The First Seven Ecumenical Councils – Their History and Theology*, (Collegeville, MN., The Liturgical Press, 1990)
IX. David W. Bercot, *A Dictionary of Early Christian Beliefs*, (Peabody, MA., Hendrickson Publishers, Inc., 1998)
X. Project Canterbury Website – (http://justus.anglican.org/resources/pc/)

CONDEMNATION OF THE ERRORS OF PASCHASIUS QUESNEL[1]
UNIGENITUS (Section 3)[2]
Dogmatic Constitution issued by Pope Clement XI on Sept. 8, 1713.

(Sec. 3) 1. What else remains for the soul that has lost God and His grace except sin and the consequences of sin, a proud poverty and a slothful indigence, that is, a general impotence for labor, for prayer, and for every good work?

2. The grace of Jesus Christ, which is the efficacious principle of every kind of good, is necessary for every good work; without it, not only is nothing done, but nothing can be done.

3. In vain, O Lord, do You command, if You do not give what you command.

4. Thus, O Lord, all things are possible to him for whom You make all things possible by effecting those same things in him.

5. When God does not soften a heart by the interior unction of His grace, exterior exhortations and graces are of no service except to harden it the more.

6. The difference between the Judaic dispensation and the Christian is this, that in the former God demanded flight from sin and a fulfillment of the Law by the sinner, leaving him in his own weakness; but in the latter. God gives the sinner what He commands, by purifying him with His grace.

7. What advantage was there for a man in the old covenant, in which God left him to his own weakness, by imposing on him His law? But what happiness is it not to be admitted to a covenant in which God gives us what He asks of us?

8. But we do not belong to the new covenant, except in so far as we are participators in that new grace which works in us that which God commands us.

9. The grace of Christ is a supreme grace, without which we can never confess Christ, and with which we never deny Him.

10. Grace is the working of the omnipotent hand of God, which nothing can hinder or retard.

11. Grace is nothing else than the omnipotent Will of God, ordering and doing what He orders.

12. When God wishes to save a soul, at whatever time and at what ever place, the undoubted effect follows the Will of God.

13. When God wishes to save a soul and touches it with the interior hand of His grace, no human will resists Him.

14. Howsoever remote from salvation an obstinate sinner is, when Jesus presents Himself to be seen by him in the salutary light of His grace, the sinner is forced to surrender himself, to have recourse to Him, and to humble himself, and to adore his Savior.

15. When God accompanies His commandment and His eternal exhortation by the unction of His Spirit and by the interior force of His grace, He works that obedience in the heart that He is seeking.

16. There are no attractions which do not yield to the attractions of grace, because nothing resists the Almighty.

17. Grace is that voice of the Father which teaches men interiorly and makes them come to Jesus Christ; whoever does not come to Him, after he has heard the exterior voice of the Son, is in no wise taught by the Father.

18. The seed of the word, which the hand of God nourishes, always brings forth its fruit.

19. The grace of God is nothing else than His omnipotent Will; this is the idea which God Himself gives us in all His Scriptures.

20. The true idea of grace is that God wishes Himself to be obeyed by us and He is obeyed; He commands, and all things are done; He speaks as the Lord, and all things are obedient to Him.

21. The grace of Jesus Christ is a strong, powerful, supreme, invincible grace, that is, the operation of the omnipotent Will, the consequence and imitation of the operation of God causing the incarnation and the resurrection of His Son.

22. The harmony of the all powerful operation of God in the heart of man with the free consent of mans will is demonstrated, therefore, to us in the Incarnation, as in the fount and archetype of all other operations of mercy and grace, all of which are as gratuitous and as dependent on God as the original operation itself.

23. God Himself has taught us the idea of the omnipotent working of His grace, signifying it by that operation which produces creatures from nothing and which restores life to the dead.

24. The right idea which the centurion had about the omnipotence of God and of Jesus Christ in healing bodies by a single act of His will, [Matt. 8:8] is an image of the idea we should have about the omnipotence of His grace in healing souls from cupidity.

25. God illumines the soul, and heals it, as well as the body, by His will only; He gives orders and He is obeyed.

26. No graces are granted except through faith.

27. Faith is the first grace and the source of all others.

28. The first grace which God grants to the sinner is the remission of sin.

29. Outside of the Church, no grace is granted.

30. All whom God wishes to save through Christ. are infallibly saved.

31. The desires of Christ always have their effect; He brings peace to the depth of hearts when He desires it for them.

32. Jesus Christ surrendered Himself to death to free forever from the hand of the exterminating angel, by His blood, the first born, that is, the elect.

33. Ah, how much one ought to renounce earthly goods and himself for this, that he may have the confidence of appropriating, so to speak, Christ Jesus to himself, His love, death, and mysteries, as St. Paul does, when he says: "He who loved me, and delivered Himself for me" [Gal. 2:20].

34. The grace of Adam produced nothing except human merit.

35. The grace of Adam is a consequence of creation and was due to his whole and sound nature.

36. The essential difference between the grace of Adam and of his state of innocence and Christian grace, is that each one would have received the first in his own person, but the second is not received except in the person of the risen Jesus Christ to whom we are united.

37. The grace of Adam by sanctifying him in himself was proportionate to him; Christian grace, by sanctifying us in Jesus Christ, is omnipotent, and worthy of the Son of God.

38. Without the grace of the Liberator, the sinner is not free except to do evil.

39. The will, which grace does not anticipate, has no light except for straying, no eagerness except to put itself in danger, no strength except to wound itself, and is capable of all evil and incapable of all good.

40. Without grace we can love nothing except to our own condemnation.

41. All knowledge of God, even natural knowledge, even in the pagan philosophers, cannot come except from God; and without grace knowledge produces nothing but presumption, vanity, and opposition to God Himself, instead of the affections of adoration, gratitude, and love.

42. The grace of Christ alone renders a man fit for the sacrifice of faith; without this there is nothing but impurity, nothing but unworthiness.

43. The first effect of baptismal grace is to make us die to sin so that our spirit, heart, and senses have no more life for sin than a dead man has for the things of the world.

44. There are but two loves, from which all our volitions and actions arise: love of God, which does all things because of God and which God rewards; and the love with which we love ourselves and the world, which does not refer to God what ought to be referred to Him, and therefore becomes evil.

45 When love of God no longer reigns in the heart of sinners, it needs must be that carnal desire reign in it and corrupt all of its actions.

46. Cupidity or charity makes the use of the senses good or evil.

47. Obedience to the law ought to flow from the source, and this source is charity. When the love of God is the interior principle of obedience and the glory of God is its end, then that is pure which appears externally; otherwise, it is but hypocrisy and false justice.

48. What else can we be except darkness, except aberration, and except sin, without the light of faith, without Christ, and without charity?

49. As there is no sin without love of ourselves, so there is no good work without love of God.

50. In vain we cry out to God: My Father, if it is not the spirit of charity which cries out.

51. Faith justifies when it operates, but it does not operate except through charity.

52. All other means of salvation are contained in faith as in their own germ and seed; but this faith does not exist apart from love and confidence.

53. Only charity in the Christian way makes (Christian actions) through a relation to God and to Jesus Christ.

54. It is charity alone that speaks to God; it alone that God hears.
55. God crowns nothing except charity; he who runs through any other incentive or any other motive, runs in vain.
56. God rewards nothing but charity; for charity alone honors God.
57. All fails a sinner, when hope fails him; and there is no hope in God, when there is no love of God.
58. Neither God nor religion exists where there is no charity.
59. The prayer of the impious is a new sin; and what God grants to them is a new judgment against them.
60. If fear of punishment alone animates penance, the more intense this is, the more it leads to despair.
61. Fear restrains nothing but the hand, but the heart is addicted to the sin as long as it is not guided by a love of justice.
62. He who does not refrain from evil except through fear of punishment, commits that evil in his heart, and is already guilty before God.
63. A baptized person is still under the law as a Jew, if he does not fulfill the law, or if he fulfills it from fear alone.
64. Good is never done under the condemnation of the law, because one sins either by doing evil or by avoiding it only through fear.
65. Moses, the prophets, priests, and doctors of the Law died without having given any son to God, since they produced only slaves through fear.
66. He who wishes to approach to God, should not come to Him with brutal passions, nor be led to Him by natural instinct, or through fear as animals, but through faith and love, as sons.
67. Servile fear does not represent God to itself except as a stern imperious, unjust, unyielding master.
68. The goodness of God has shortened the road to salvation, by enclosing all in faith and in prayers.
69. Faith, practice of it increase, and reward of faith, all are a gift of the pure liberality of God.
70. Never does God afflict the innocent; and afflictions always serve either to punish the sin or to purify the sinner.
71. For the preservation of himself man can dispense himself from that law which God established for his use.
72. A mark of the Christian Church is that it is catholic, embracing all the angels of heaven, all the elect and the just on earth, and of all times
73. What is the Church except an assembly of the sons of God abiding in His bosom, adopted in Christ, subsisting in His person, redeemed by His blood, living in His spirit, acting through His grace, and awaiting the grace of the future life?
74. The Church or the whole Christ has the Incarnate Word as head but all the saints as members.
75. The Church is one single man composed of many members, of which Christ is the head, the life, the subsistence and the person- it is one single Christ composed of many saints, of whom He is the sanctifier
76. There is nothing more spacious than the Church of God; because all the elect and the just of all ages comprise it.
77. He who does not lead a life worthy of a son of God and a member of Christ, ceases interiorly to have God as a Father and Christ as a head.
78. One is separated from the chosen people, whose figure was the Jewish people, and whose head is Jesus Christ, both by not living according to the Gospel and by not believing in the Gospel.
79. It is useful and necessary at all times, in all places, and for every kind of person, to study and to know the spirit, the piety, and the mysteries of Sacred Scripture.
80. The reading of Sacred Scripture is for all.
81. The sacred obscurity of the Word of God is no reason for the laity to dispense themselves from reading it.
82. The Lord's Day ought to be sanctified by Christians with readings of pious works and above all of the Holy Scriptures. It is harmful for a Christian to wish to withdraw from this reading.
83. It is an illusion to persuade oneself that knowledge of the mysteries of religion should not be communicated to women by the reading of Sacred Scriptures. Not from the simplicity of women, but from the proud knowledge of men has arisen the abuse of the Scriptures and have heresies been born.
84. To snatch away from the hands of Christians the New Testament, or to hold it closed against them by taking away from them the means of understanding it, is to close for them the mouth of Christ.

85. To forbid Christians to read Sacred Scripture, especially the Gospels, is to forbid the use of light to the sons of light, and to cause them to suffer a kind of excommunication.

86. To snatch from the simple people this consolation of joining their voice to the voice of the whole Church is a custom contrary to the apostolic practice and to the intention of God.

87. A method full of wisdom light, and charity is to give souls time for bearing with humility. and for experiencing their state of sin, for seeking the spirit of penance and contrition, and for beginning at least to satisfy the justice of God, before they are reconciled.

88. We are ignorant of what sin is and of what true penance is, when we wish to be restored at once to the possession of the goods of which sin has despoiled us, and when we refuse to endure the confusion of that separation.

89. The fourteenth step in the conversion of a sinner is that, after he has already been reconciled, he has the right of assisting at the Sacrifice of the Church.

90. The Church has the authority to excommunicate, so that it may exercise it through the first pastors with the consent, at least presumed, of the whole body.

91. The fear of an unjust excommunication should never hinder us from fulfilling our duty; never are we separated from the Church, even when by the wickedness of men we seem to be expelled from it, as long as we are attached to God, to Jesus Christ, and to the Church herself by charity.

92. To suffer in peace an excommunication and an unjust anathema rather than betray truth, is to imitate St. Paul; far be it from rebelling against authority or of destroying unity.

93 Jesus sometimes heals the wounds which the precipitous haste of the first pastors inflicted without His command. Jesus restored what they, with unconsidered zeal, cut off.

94. Nothing engenders a worse opinion of the Church among her enemies than to see exercised there an absolute rule over the faith of the faithful, and to see divisions fostered because of matters, which do not violate faith or morals.

95. Truths have descended to this, that they are, as it were, a foreign tongue to most Christians, and the manner of preaching them is, as it were, an unknown idiom, so remote is the manner of preaching from the simplicity of the apostles. and so much above the common grasp of the faithful;

nor is there sufficient advertence to the fact that this defect is one of the greatest visible signs of the weakening of the Church and of the wrath of God on His sons.

96. God permits that all powers be opposed to the preachers of truth, so that its victory cannot be attributed to anyone except to divine grace.

97. Too often it happens that those members, who are united to the Church more holily and more strictly, are looked down upon, and treated as if they were unworthy of being in the Church, or as if they were separated from Her; but, "the just man liveth by faith" [Rom. 1:17], and not by the opinion of men.

98. The state of persecution and of punishment which anyone endures as a disgraceful and impious heretic, is generally the final trial and is especially meritorious, inasmuch as it makes a man more conformable to Jesus Christ.

99. Stubbornness, investigation, and obstinacy in being unwilling either to examine something or to acknowledge that one has been deceived daily changes into an odor, as it were, of death, for many people, that which God has placed in His Church to be an odor of life within it, for instance, good books, instructions, holy examples, etc.

100. Deplorable is the time in which God is believed to be honored by persecution of the truth and its disciples! This time has come.... To be considered and treated by the ministers of religion as impious and unworthy of all commerce with God, as a putrid member capable of corrupting everything in the society of saints, is to pious men a more terrible death than the death of the body. In vain does anyone flatter himself on the purity of his intentions and on a certain zeal for religion, when he persecutes honest men with fire and sword, if he is blinded by his own passion or carried away by that of another on account of which he does not want to examine anything. We frequently believe that we arc sacrificing an impious man to God, when we are sacrificing a servant of God to the devil.

101. Nothing is more opposed to the spirit of God and to the doctrine of Jesus Christ than to swear common oaths in Church, because this is to multiply occasions of perjury, to lay snares for the weak and inexperienced, and to cause the name and truth of God to serve sometimes the plan of the wicked.

Declared and condemned as false, captious, evil-sounding, offensive to pious ears, scandalous, pernicious, rash, injurious to the Church and her practice, insulting not only to the Church but also the secular powers seditious, impious, blasphemous, suspected of heresy, and smacking of heresy itself, and, besides, favoring heretics and heresies, and also schisms, erroneous, close to heresy, many times condemned, and finally heretical, clearly renewing many heresies respectively and most especially those which are contained in the infamous propositions of Jansen, and indeed accepted in that sense in which these have been condemned.

INNOCENT XIII 1721-1724 BENEDICT XIII 1724-1730 CLEMENT XII 1730-1740

---

1 DuPl III, II 462 ff.: coll. Viva II I ff.; CIC Rcht II 140 ff.; BR(T) 21, 569 b ff.; MBR 8, 119 a ff. Variant, doubtful, and corrected readings are according to the first Gallic text which DuPl, l.c., presents-Paschasius Quesnel was born on July 14, 1634. After completing his studies in the Sorbonne in 1657, he entered the Congregation of the Oratory; but because of his zeal for the heresy of Jansenism, he was forced to leave the congregation. His book, "Reflections morales," was condemned, to which the Constitution, "Unigenitus," is related. Shortly before his death on Dec. 2, 1719, he made a profession of faith publicly [Hrt, sec. rec. II2 822 ff]. 2 This dogmatic constitution was confirmed by the same Clement XI in the Bull "Pastoralis Officii" (Aug. 28, 1718) against the Appellantes, in which he declares that certain Catholics "who did not accept the Bull "Unigenitus" were clearly outside the bosom of the Roman Church; by Innocent XIII in a decree published on Jan. 8, 1722; by Benedict XIII and the Roman Synod in 1725; by Benedict XIV in the encyclical, "Ex omnibus Christiani orbis regionibus" on Oct. 16, 1756; it was accepted by the Gallic clergy in assemblies in 1723, 1726, 1730, by the councils of Avignon 1725 and Ebred, 1727, and by the whole Catholic world.

Ligue des Catholiques de France
104 RUE DE RICHELIEI
Paris
Secretariat General

BULL OF HIS HOLINESS
PATRIARCH IGNATIUS PETER III

OF THE APOSTOLIC SEE OF ANTIOCH AND THE EAST
FOR THE CONSECRATION OF ARCHBISHOP VILATTE

(TRANSLATED FROM THE SYRIAC)

In the name of the Essential, Eternal, Self-existing, Almighty God, His servant, Ignatius Pater [sic] III, Patriarch of the Apostolic See of Antioch and the East.

We, the humble servant of God, hereby allow the consecration by the Holy Ghost of the Priest Joseph Rene Vilatte, elected for Archepiscopal dignity, Archbishop Metropolitan, in the name of Mar Thimotheus, for the church of the Mother of God in Dyckesville, Wisconsin, United States, and other churches in the Archdiocese of America, viz, the churches adhering to the Orthodox Faith, in the name of the Father, Amen, of the Son, Amen, and of the Living Holy Ghost, Amen.

We stand up before God's majesty, and, raising up our hands towards His grace, pray that the Holy Ghost may descend upon him, as He did upon the Apostles at the time of the ascension of our Lord Jesus Christ, by whom they were made Patriarchs[,] Bischops [sic] and Priests, and were authorised to bind and loose, as written by St. Matthew.

We, therefore, by virtue of our authority received from God, authorise him to bind and loose, and, elevating our voice, we offer thanks to God, and exclaim, "Kyrie eleison, Kyrie eleison, Kyrie eleison." Again, we pray to God to grant him cheer of face before His throne of majesty, and that at all times for ever and ever.

Given on the seventeenth of Conoon Kadmayo, of the year of our Lord, eighteen hundred and ninety one (corresponding to twenty-ninth of December, eighteen hundred and ninety-one), from the Patriarchal Palace of the monastery of Mardin.

(Seal) IGNATIUS PETER III

(Seal) Mar DIONYSIUS,
Metropolitan of Malabar

True translation E.M. Philip
Secretary to the Metropolitan of Malabar
Syrian Seminary
(Seal)

The Place of the Old Catholics in the Work of Unity by the Rev. C. B. Moss.

The Old Catholic churches are seven small autocephalous churches in communion with the ancient see of Utrecht, which was founded by St. Willibrord in 697, and was excommunicated by Rome early in the eighteenth century. Their separate position is the result of three movements in different periods and countries; the struggle between the See of Utrecht and the Jesuits; the revolt in Germany and other countries against the Vatican Council; later "Los von Rom" movements in South-Eastern Europe and in America.

The Old Catholic movement has always received much sympathy both from Orthodox and from Anglican authorities. The Oecumenical Patriarch Joachim II. sent his last message to his Anglican friends not to forget the Old Catholics: and successive Lambeth Conferences, ever since 1878, have offered special privileges to Old Catholics deprived of the ministry of their own clergy.

The International Congress of the Old Catholic Churches meets about every three years. The Bishops meet in private, and decide questions affecting the whole Communion: the clergy and laity, with visitors from other communions, meet in public. It is like a Lambeth Conference and a Church Congress combined. Last summer the Congress was held at Utrecht, the mother-city of the Old Catholic Churches. At the Pontifical High Mass in St. Gertrude's Cathedral, with which the Congress opened, the Archbishop and his assistants wore fifteenth-century vestments which have survived in the Church of Utrecht from the age of Thomas a Kempis and Erasmus. A visit was paid by the members of the Congress to the tomb of Van Espen, the great canonist and ardent defender of the rights of the See of Utrecht, at Amersfoort, and to the theological seminary in that city, now two centuries old. A series of tableaux was given in the theatre, illustrating the history of the See of Utrecht from the mission of St. Willibrord, of whom the present Archbishop, Mgr. Francis Kenninck, is the canonical successor, to modern times. The visitors to this Congress included priests representing the Greek, Bulgarian, English, and American Churches.

The Old Catholics, like the Orthodox churches, accept the Seven Councils and the Seven Sacraments, but not the Papal Supremacy or the "Filioque" clause. They resemble the Anglican churches in being modern and critical, and in certain points of discipline: e.g., the clergy of all orders are permitted to marry after ordination. It is natural that Utrecht should be regarded as a bridge between Constantinople and Canterbury, with each of which if. has points of contact. And yet this is not quite the real place of the Old Catholic churches in the work of unity.

It is clear that the dogmatic basis of the re-united Church of the future must be Orthodox, for it is fantastic to suppose that the dogmatic basis of Orthodoxy can be changed, though it may be explained. But its Eastern forms are not of universal obligation. St. Cyprian and St. Augustine are Orthodox saints as well as St. Athanasius and St. Basil. If Orthodoxy were opposed to the Latin element in Christianity as such, it would have no claim to be a universal religion.

We Anglicans are often told that we are "Western." In a sense, of course, we are. But the phrase is a misleading half-truth. It is like saying that Englishmen are Teutons, or that the United States is of English origin. The English Church is, of course, of Latin origin (though we must not forget the important work of the Greek Archbishop Theodore), but she has developed a character of her own. The characteristic Anglican theologians, such as Hooker and Butler, Westcott and Moberly, belong to a different world from the great stream of Latin theology which extends from Tertullian to Cardinal Mercier. And what is true of the theologians is still more true of the laity. The idea of a fundamental division of the world into "Eastern" and "Western" (which means Greek and Latin), which befogs the mind of the man trained in early church history, does not exist for the ordinary Englishman. He knows that in many ways the Mediterranean peoples are more like one another than he is like any of them. The re-union between Constantinople and Canterbury for which we work and pray is not a re-union of "East" and "West." Anglicans are not non-Papal Latins. We represent a third development of Catholic Christianity, and are as different from Latins (apart altogether from Protestant infiltration) as Latins are from "Easterns."

But though we are not non-Papal Latins, that is just what the Old-Catholics are. Though not Latins in speech (for the Old Catholic movement never took root in France, Italy, or the Peninsula), they are Latins in rite, in theology, in canon law. Few and weak though they are, they are the heirs of a great tradition, the tradition of opposition within Latin Christendom to the Papal claims, of Gerson and Bossuet, Pascal and Van Espen, Hebronius and Strossmayer. Gallicanism, indeed, was doomed, once it had consented, at that ill-omened Council of Constance, stained for ever by the broken safe-conduct of John Huss, to elect the new Pope before proceeding to the reform of the Church. For the struggle between the Pope, who is always there, and the Council, which can only meet occasionally, could end in but one way: and the triumph of Martin V. led inevitably to the Vatican Decrees of Pius IX. There was only one real alternative to Ultramontanism, the autocephaly of national churches: which Gallicanism never ventured to demand, but which the Anglican and Old Catholic churches have won, at the cost, it is true, of schism and many other evils.

So we look to the Old Catholic churches to represent, in the greater Orthodox Church of the future, that Latin element which neither Constantinople nor Canterbury can supply. And therefore it is of the utmost importance that there should be no interference with their independence, or disturbance, even unconscious, of their Latin traditions, from either the Anglican or from the Eastern side.

But there is another service to Christendom which the Old Catholics may possibly be able to perform hereafter. If their traditions are Latin, the speech of most of them is German or Dutch. They may be able to interpret the Orthodox Faith to the Teutonic nations of the Continent. The famous correspondence between Leibniz and Bossuet with a view to re-union broke down because Leibniz discovered, to his dismay, that even the Gallican Bossuet would not listen to his proposal to go behind the Council of Trent. "Protestants," he writes, "as well as all those who really love the honour of God and the welfare of the Church, are bound to reject such a council for ever: if it was regarded as Oecumenical we could no longer trust in Oecumenical Councils nor in the stable tradition of antiquity. There could be no greater rashness and folly than to utter an anathema against the whole ancient Church, arising as it does from a mere hatred of the Protestants, without reason or necessity." These are the words of the man who was ready to concede more to Rome than any other Protestant leader since the Reformation.

Now the Old Catholics have done what Bossuet would not do: they have gone behind Trent. Therefore, should any successor to Leibniz arise among the Lutherans in our day, the Old Catholics are the natural bridge by which he might seek union, not, indeed, with Rome, but with Constantinople.

As we look to the Old Catholics to supply the Latin element in the Orthodox Church of the future, so we also look to them to interpret the Orthodox Faith to Germany, Holland and Scandinavia.

For Orthodoxy is not necessarily Greek or Slavonic, any more than Anglicanism is necessarily English or American. We look forward to a time, perhaps not very remote, when Orthodox doctrine (though not necessarily Byzantine ritual, beautiful and splendid though it is) shall be spread throughout both the English-speaking and the German-speaking world, as the basis of a greater Orthodox Church, no longer merely "Eastern," but "Northern," as well; when the children of Theodore, Willibrord, and Boniface, shall be perfected together with those of Athanasius and Chrysostom, Cyril and Methodius, "in the same mind and in the same judgment" (I Cor., i, 10.)

The Place of the Old Catholics in the Work of Unity by the Rev. C. B. Moss.
The Christian East, Winter, 1928, pp. 167-170.

The New Schaff-Herzog Encyclopedia of Religious Knowledge, Vol XIII: Index
by
Philip Schaff

OLD CATHOLICS.

The Old Catholic Church owes its origin to certain Roman Catholics who refused to accept the decree of the Vatican Council of 1870 (q.v.) affirming the infallibility of the pope when speaking ex cathedra. The decree had been fiercely debated and opposed by a considerable minority of the bishops present at the council, their arguments being based upon the early history of the Church and its fundamental faith and usages as declared by the ecumenical councils. A further charge made by the minority was that freedom of discussion had not prevailed at the council and that final action was forced. Of this minority only a few, however, persisted in the logical course indicated by their position. The organization of the opposition after the issuance of the decree was made at a meeting at

Nuremberg, Aug. 27, 1870, of professors from Bonn, Breslau, Bmunsberg, Munich, Munster, Prague, W 9rzburg, and other places, who, under the leadership of Johann Josef Ignaz von D6llinger (q.v.), declared against the decree. A gathering of laymen at KOnigswinter in September of the same year resolved that: " Considering that the council . . . did not deliberate in perfect freedom, . . . the undersigned Catholics [1,359 in number] do not recognize the decrees concerning the absolute power of the pope and his infallibility as the decision of an ecumenical council, but rather reject them as innovations in direct contradiction to the uniform faith of the Church." Of the dissenting minority spoken of above Bishop Hefele was the last to submit (April, 1871). Ecclesiastical pressure was brought upon the dissenting professors, and those who continued in opposition were excommunicated. The necessity was seen for an organization to protect the scattered clergy who adhered to the position of the minority, and a congress was held at Munich Sept. 22-24, 1871, with Prof. J. F. von Schulte of Bonn presiding, at which the conclusions of the preceding gatherings mentioned were endorsed, the direction the movement should take was decided, and measures were taken for the cure of souls. The organization of congregations in various places followed. The second congress was held at Cologn- Sept. 20, 1872, provision was made for the election of a bishop, who was chosen on June 4, 1873, the choice falling on Joseph Hubert Reinkens (q.v.), professor of theology at Breslau, who received consecration at Rotterdam from the Jansenist Bishop Heycamp of Deventer, his recognition by the king of Prussia following on Sept. 17 of the same year, and by other German princes a little later. At this congress provision was made for the government of the church by a Synodical board of clerical and lay members. The third congress was held at Constance in Sept., 1873. Thereafter the congresses were regularly held, but their function was limited to general discussions for the general good, provision for the specific care of the church being committed to the synod, which was organized.

The first synod was held at Bonn, 1874, and successive synods shaped the polity and life of the church. The possibility of union with the Protestant Church was not overlooked. A Faith catechism and a manual of instruction and were issued, recognizing only those practices and doctrines which were deemed apostolic. Auricular confession was made voluntary, and absolution was regarded as a ceremonial declaration made by the priest as a servant of Jesus Christ. Christ, " the son of God in the sense that he is of the same essence with the Father," is the head of the church, which latter is defined as the invisible body including all who have part in salvation through faith in Christ. The Apostles' Creed is employed in all services except the mass, where the Nicene Creed is used. Attempts were made to do away with abuses arising from penance, fasts and festivals, the celibacy of priests, and various matters financial, while the use of the German language has been so extended as to cover the entire service. A board of clerics and laymen has been made an organ of church direction, with the bishop as president and a layman as vice-president. The synod is the representative body, constituted of the bishop, president exofecio, the board just named, and the priests and deputies of the congregation; its powers are legislative, judicial, disciplinary, and administrative. Pastors and assistant pastors are chosen by the congregations (since 1878), with Episcopal approval, except in the case of benefices. Trial for lighter offenses is before the bishop or bishop and board, for more serious cases of offense before a synod court, with procedure based upon the German code. For parish purposes a church board exists, composed of the pastor and a body of councilors

chosen for three years by the congregation. Candidates are ordained by the bishop after examination, which is preceded by the regular course in the universities. Various funds exist for supporting the work of the church.
II. In Other European Countries: The priests who in Switzerland refused the Vatican decrees adopted a constitution for " The Christian Catholic Church of Switzerland " similar to that of the Old Catholics of Germany. The first synod was held at Olten in June, 1875, and Eduard Herzog (q.v.), professor of Catholic theology at Bern, was elected bishop in June, 1876. The general course of development was similar to that in Germany; communion in both kinds was made optional, and regulations for the festivals and observances were adopted.

In Austria earlier efforts to organize Old Catholics were opposed by the upper house of parliament and the government. In 1875 governmental opposition was withdrawn, and in 1876 a meeting of delegates was held at Vienna, and legal recognition was given to the Old Catholic Church Oct. 18, 1877. At a provisional synod at Vienna in July, 1879, the reforms of the church in Germany and Switzerland were accepted. The first regular synod was held in June, 1880, when five priests and a number of laymen attended. At the twentieth synod in Vienna in 1900 sixty members were present, and there were reported 16,885 members, and other details of a remarkable growth were presented. In Italy the movement showed less vigor than in the other countries named above, and it was not till 1875 that delegates from a number of congregations met at Naples and elected Luigi Proto Giurlo bishop of the National Catholic Church. In France an active interest was taken by Charles Jean Marie Augustin Hyacinth Loyson (q.v.) and the Abb6 Michaud, and a congregation was formed in Paris in 1878 to which the ministrations of bishops of Holland, Switzerland, and England were given at various times. A temporary bishop was chosen in 1888 in the person of Henry Laseelles Jenner. In Russia several communities of Bohemians attached themselves to the Old Catholic movement, obtained recognition, and also support from the State for three priests. In 1880 permission was gained for a conference to frame a constitution for permanent organization. A number of prelates of the Orthodox Church have shown sympathy with the movement and have attended the international congresses. The organization of the Old Catholic
Church in England was not perfected till 1908, when A. N. Mathew was elected bishop, secured the recognition of the Old Catholic Church of Holland, and was consecrated at Utrecht Apr. 28, 1908, having in his diocese seventeen priests.
In the United States: The discontent over the Vatican decrees in the United States was somewhat slower in taking organized form. Joseph Rena Villatte, a priest of French Canadian ancestry, who had sustained various relations in connection with various Protestant ties for mission work among foreign (Polish) populations in Wisconsin, had received Catholic ordination from Bishop Herzog of the Church. Swiss Christian Catholic Church (ut sup.) and also received Episcopal consecration in 1892 from Archbishop Alvarez of India, Ceylon, and Goa. But the right of Alvarez to per form episcopal acts was under question, and the consecration of Villatte was not recognized by the Old Catholic bishops of Europe or by the Protestant Episcopalian bishops in the United States. Hence the attempts made by Villatte to found an Old Catholic Church in the United States had no permanent result. More successful has been the work among the Polish immigrants to this country, people of this nationality coming here with a lively dissatisfaction with the course of the Roman Catholic Church in their own land. Many of them had no ecclesiastical relations at all, and a movement was begun by Anthony Koslowaki (d. Jan. 14, 1907), a Pole of Italian education, who became rector of a Polish congregation in Chicago in 1893. The next year he withdrew from the Roman Catholic communion and became a leader in the reform movement, was elected a bishop, and received consecration from the Old Catholic bishop of Switzerland at Bern, Switzerland, in 1897, founding the Independent (Polish) Catholic Church. The growth of the organization was remarkable; congregations were established in Chicago, Baltimore, Philadelphia, Cleveland, Buffalo, Jersey City, Fall River, Mass., and Wilkesbarre, Pa.; and in 1902 it re ported 22 priests, 10 sisters, 26 congregations, 80,000 adherents, 26 schools with 3,000 attendants, 26 Sunday-schools, and 31 buildings. It had, besides, an educational institution with grammar and high school and industrial departments in Chicago, and connected with it a hospital and dispensary and a home for the aged. Overtures were made in 1902 to the Protestant Episcopal Church of the United States for recognition and intercommunion on the basis of the Lambeth " Quadrilateral " (see LAMBETH ARTICLES; LAMBETH CONFERENCE), but beyond referring the matter to a committee no definite action has been taken. In the overtures the object of the organization was stated as the wish to serve those who cannot intelligently take part in

worship Conducted in the English tongue, and allegiance was pledged to the Old Catholic Synod of Europe until such time as the church shall be received by the Protestant Episcopal Church as an affiliated body.

The disposition to separate from the Roman Catholic Church illustrated by the formation of the Polish organization just described manifested itself also among Bohemians and others of Slavic race in America. A number of independent congregations nucleated in several cities. It was felt that these should be united under episcopal administration, and as the Independent Catholic (Polish) Catholic Church desired to restrict its work to Poles, a separate organization seemed necessary. The ad vice of the Old Catholic bishops of Utrecht and Switzerland was asked, and in consequence of their advice, taking into account the largeness of the country and the possibility of three or four Old Catholic dioceses, the National Catholic Church was organized, with Jan F. Tichy as Episcopal administrator (appointed by the bishop of Utrecht). This Church " is formed upon the same basis as the mother Church in Switzerland," this including theoretical as well as practical matters. Its attitude is avowedly friendly toward the Polish organization and to the Protestant Episcopal Church. It derives its apostolic succession from the Church in Holland. It reported in 1906, 9 churches and 11 missions in the United States and Canada, 7 priests, and about 15,000 members. It is incorporated in Ohio, and has a cathedral and other buildings in Cleveland with property valued at about $20,000. Bulletin 103 of the United States Census (Religious Bodies) gives the Polish National Church in America 24 priests, 24 ministers, 15,473 communicants, and church property valued at $494,700.

IV. Statistics and the Congresses: In 1900 there were reported 57 active clergy and 13,079 communicants in Germany; approximately 40 parishes in Switzerland; 24 parishes and 16,885 members in Austria; and 21 parishes in Holland, where it possessed also the Amerafoort theological seminary; a few churches existed in Italy, the movement was represented in France, and attempts had been made in Portugal and Spain. In 1904 the German states of Prussia, Bavaria, Baden, and Hesse had 65 clergy, 11,201 communicants, and 1,946 children receiving instruction in the schools. In 1878 the Old Catholics of Europe began holding their synods (for business) and their general congresses (for discussion) in different years. Congresses have been held at Cologne 1891, Lucerne 1892, Rotterdam 1894, Vienna 1897, and Bonn 1902. At these meetings representatives have at different times been present from the Protestant Episcopal Church of the United States, the Russian Church, the Petite Itglise of France, the Church of England. The subjects for discussion have taken a wide range, including the matter of international churches and the establishment of an international theological faculty, the dissemination of Old Catholic literature, the propaganda among the Slavic populations, the formation of societies for religious, educational, and social objects, practical matters such as the establishment of a fund for the support of priests joining the movement until they can be settled at work, and the Z08 von Rom movement (q.v.).

JANSEHIST CHURCH IN HOLLAND. Contributory Causes of the Schism of 1702 (§ 1). Its Immediate Occasion (§ 2). History (§ 3). Differences from the Roman Catholic Church (§ 4).

The doctrines of Jansenism (see JANSEN, COR NELIU9, JANBENIBM) left no permanent trace in Belgium or in France, but in Holland there has been for more than two centuries a church popularly called Jansenist. Its adherents reject the name, of the rightly calling themselves the Old Schism Catholic Church of Holland, since the schism among the Dutch Roman Catholics in 1702, to which they owe their origin, sprang from the adherence of the Dutch clergy to the privileges of their church rather than from dogmatic principles. The first bishop in Holland was Willibrord (q.v.), consecrated bishop of Utrecht by Pope Sergius I. in 695. Among his successors were not a few who opposed the growing tendency to regard the pope as the unrestricted governor of all Christendom. The bishop of Utrecht was originally chosen by the clergy, and in 1145 the Emperor Conrad III, confirmed the right to the chapter of St. Martin's Cathedral. The choice was not always accepted by Rome. In 1559 in accordance with the wish of Philip II. of Spain, then ruler of the Netherlands, the pope elevated Utrecht to the rank of an archbishopric with five suffragan sees, and it was then agreed by pope and king that the latter should select the bishops, to be confirmed by the pope. Nine years later the War of Liberation broke out, lasting for eighty years, and involved the Roman Catholics in many difficulties. Though they joined. with the Protestants in fighting against the Spanish yoke, they were mistrusted, and about 1573 the public exercise of Catholic worship was forbidden-a prohibition which remained in force till the revolution of 1795. As the incumbents of the episcopal sees died, it was found difficult to fill their places. Sasbold Vosmeer, chosen general vicar by the Utrecht chapter in 1583, after the death of the archbishop in 1580, was consecrated archbishop by the pope in 1602, but with the title archbishop of Philippi. His successors were chosen and consecrated in the same way. Under the fifth of them, Petrus Codde (consecrated 1689), occurred the schism.

More formidable opponents than the Protestants had appeared against the Roman Catholic clergy of Holland. During the turbulent conditions of the long war the country Immediate had been invaded by " regular " clergy especially by the Jesuits after 1590, who accused the Dutch clergy of the Jansenistic heresy. In 1697, during the negotiations of peace at Ryswik, there appeared an anonymous treatise in French, soon afterward also in Latin, and some years later in Dutch, under the title " Short Memorial concerning the Condition and Progress of Jansenism in Holland." Some copies fell into the hands of Codde, who hastened to send the book to Rome with an apology. He was declared innocent in Rome, although there was no end of insinuations. Since Alexander VII. had issued his constitution against the so-called five theses of Jansen in 1656, the accusation implied that the accused was suspected of agreeing with the five condemned theses, or of refusing to believe that Jansen had taught those theses in his Augustinus, and thereby given rise to the heresy condemned by the church. Codde and his subordinate ecclesiastics could easily defend themselves against the charge of agreeing with the content of the condemned theses, although the former did not express himself on the question whether Jansen had really taught them or not. But since the decision of Alexander, this point involved the absolute supremacy and infallibility of the pope, and the Jesuits were intent upon having this question decided. Codde was summoned to Rome in 1700, and in 1702 was declared guilty of heresy. There was great consternation in Holland when it was learned that he had been dismissed from office, and still more when Theodor de Kock, his opponent, was appointed general vicar. The estates took the part of Codde and forced his opponents to let him return to Holland, where he arrived in 1703. The question now was, what attitude would Codde, the Dutch clergy, and the Utrecht chapter assume. If they accepted Codde's dismissal, the independence of the Utrecht church was necessarily abolished. Codde himself, from love of peace, remained until his death in a passive attitude, steadfastly asserting his rights and those of his church, but refraining from exercising them.

A large party of the Dutch' clergy and laity, however, remained faithful to him, although another part followed De Kock. Thus Codde's dismissal led to a schism in the Dutch Roman Catholic Church which has never been healed. It was to be expected that the church of the Jansenists, as Codde's party was now called, would decrease in numbers after Rome had spoken. Owing to the lack of higher ecclesiastics, the church of Utrecht was on the point of extinction, when aid came in an unexpected manner. Several French clergymen who refused to sign the bull Unigenitus in 1713 (see JANSEN, CORNELIUS, JANSENISM) sought refuge on Dutch soil. Moreover, in 1719, Dom Maria Varlet (chosen bishop of Babylon in 1718 and consecrated as bishop of Ascalon Feb. 19, 1719) spent some time in Amsterdam before he undertook his journey to the Orient. In Amsterdam be he came acquainted with ecclesiastics of the Old Catholic Church and was active in their behalf. He had hardly reached the Orient when the pope suspended him as a Jansenist. He then returned to Holland, where the Utrecht chapter in 1723 had elected Cornelis Steenoven as archbishop to prevent the extinction of the Old Catholic Church. In 1724 Bishop Varlet consecrated him. The pope, of course, immediately put Steenoven under the ban, but the Utrecht church was saved from extinction. Steenoven died in 1725, and was succeeded by Barchman Wuytiers (d. 1733), who was followed by Theodor van der Croon (d. 1739), both consecrated by Varlet. The Utrecht church soon recognized the danger of making its continuance dependent upon the life of a single bishop, and consequently Hieronymus de Bock was consecrated bishop of Haarlem in 1742, and B. J. Bijevelt bishop of Deventer in 1758. Several attempts to reconcile the pope failed. A serious danger threatened the Old Catholic Church in Holland under the administration of the Roman Catholic king, Louis Bonaparte (1806-10), and under the regime of Emperor Napoleon (1810-13), who contemplated prohibiting the election of a new Old Catholic bishop; but this danger passed with the restitution of the independence of Holland, and in 1814 W. van Os was elected archbishop of Utrecht, and in 1819 Johannes Bon bishop of Haarlem (see EPISCOPACY, III.). The difficulties which threatened the church under King William I. and King William IL, who desired to establish a concordat with the pope, passed as soon as the agreement failed. The law concerning church associations enacted in 1853 assured entire freedom to all ecclesiastical organizations, including the Old Catholics. In this way the small church has gradually increased its members from 5,000 to almost 8,000, and its parishes from twenty-five to twenty six. It is not strange that the Old Catholic bishops disapproved the dogma of the Immaculate Conception in 1854, and that of papal infallibility in 1870. The chief points of difference between the Old Catholics of Holland and their Roman Catholic opponents are the following:

(1) The Old Catholic Church considers the deposition of Archbishop Codde illegal, and asserts that, in spite of the Reformation of the sixteenth century and its Church the Roman Catholic Church has existed without interruption, and has continuously retained its right to administer its own affairs as a national church, independent of the church in Rome.

(2) It refuses to sign the formula of Pope Alexander VII., unless permitted to make a distinction between a signature quoad jua and quond fnctum; namely, between the question whether the five incriminated theses were heretical, and the question whether Jansen had taught them in a heretical sense.

(3) It rejects the bull Unigenitus, since this bull val idates the moral system of the Jesuits for the whole Roman Catholic Church. The importance of the Old Catholic Church of Holland for all Roman Catholic Christendom lies not only in the fact that it is a monument of the spirit of the earlier centuries, but also in the fact that it has entered into relations with the Old Catholic movement in Germany and Switzerland. When the Old Catholic spirit was aroused in Germany in opposition to the dogma of infallibility in 1870, and the necessity of a bishop for the newly organized Old Catholic Church was felt, it was H. Heykamp, the Old Catholic bishop of Deventer, who, in 1873, consecrated J. H. Reinkena bishop of the German Old Catholics. See OLD CATHOLICS. (J. A. GE'RTH VAN WIJK.)

BIBLIOGRAPHY: C, P. HOy71Ck a Papendreeht, Hitt. ecclesiae Uitralectinae, Mechlin, 1725; T. Baekhusius, BewijrSchrift, 3 vole., Utrecht, 17230; M. G. Dupao de Bellegarde, Hiet, abr4g6e de l'Epi%ae m0ropoZitaine d'Utreeht, ib. 1852 J. W. Neale, Hint. of the so-called Janaeniat Church of Holland, London 1858; R. Bennink Janaeonius, Oeechiedenia der Oud-RoomacA-KathoZieke Kerk in Nederland, The Hague, 1870; F. Nippold, Die r6miach-katholiache Kirche . der Niederlande, Leipeie, 1877; J. A. van Beek, Geschiedenis der hollandache Kerk, Rotterdam, 1886; Neerlsndia Catholics, Utrecht, 1888; J. do Huller, Bijdrape tot de peachiedenie van hot Utrechtachs 3chisma, The Hague, 1892; W. P. C. Knuttel, Ds Toealand der nederlandache Katholieken, 2 vote., ib. 1892-94; J. Meyhoffer, Le Msrtyrdope Protestant des Paya-Bas, 1¢88-1697, The Hague, 1907. The literature of the church is given by J. A. van Beek, Lijat roan taeken uitpsuen in de Oud-KatJwlieke Kerk, 3 vole., Rotterdam, 1892-93. Much of the literature under JAII6ENIaM is pertinent, e.g., the work of Tregellee.

www.ingramcontent.com/pod-product-compliance
Lightning Source LLC
Chambersburg PA
CBHW081350040426
42450CB00015B/3382